FINDING DADDY

A memoir of a murder,
survival, and a 911 operator's
worst nightmare

Shiela Hanna-Wiles with Katie Clark Vecchio

FINDING DADDY

Shiela Hanna-Wiles with Katie Clark Vecchio

FINDING DADDY

Copyright @ 2014 Sheila Hanna-Wiles

Library of Congress Cataloging-in-Publication Data

Hanna-Wiles, Sheila.
  Finding Daddy : survival and hope through a 911 telecommunicator's nightmare / Sheila Hanna-Wiles with Katie Clark Vecchio.
    pages cm
  ISBN 978-0-9852478-3-6 (paperback : alkaline paper)
  1. Hanna-Wiles, Sheila. 2. Hanna-Wiles, Sheila--Family. 3. Murder--South Carolina--Anderson County. 4. Burglary--South Carolina--Anderson County. 5. Fathers--South Carolina--Anderson County--Death. 6. Police dispatchers--South Carolina--Anderson County--Biography. 7. Emergency communication systems--South Carolina--Anderson County. 8. Married people--South Carolina--Anderson County--Biography. 9. Mothers and sons--South Carolina--Anderson County--Biography. I. Vecchio, Katie Clark. II. Title.
  HV6533.S6H36 2014
  364.152'3092--dc23
                    2014003240

For inquiries about volume orders, please contact:

TitleTown Publishing LLC
PO Box 12093
Green Bay, WI 54307
920.737.8051
titletownpublishing.com

Editor: Amanda Bindel
Cover Design: Michael Short
Interior Layout and Design: Megan Trank and Michael Short

Published in the United States by TitleTown Publishing
www.titletownpublishing.com

Distributed by Midpoint Trade Books
www.midpointtrade.com

Printed in the United States of America

I would like to dedicate this book first to my Heavenly Father for giving me the strength, guidance, and wisdom to overcome and find the good from something so bad. And in memory of my earthly father, Charlton "Stoney" Parnell. Daddy, thank you for giving me the vision and purpose behind sharing my story. Your perseverance in seeing this project happen allowed the boys and me an opportunity, for the first time, to share with each other our fears, hopes, and memories of Johnny. A lot of healing took place during this journey and it all came from your persistence on writing this book. I love you and miss you more than words could say!
—*Sheila Hanna-Wiles*

I dedicate this book to justice and those who have lost loved ones to murder.
—*Katie Clark Vecchio*

CONTENTS

CHAPTER 1

THEY MIGHT STILL
BE HERE

U NTIL THAT DAY, we'd never given any thought to how remote our house was. It had always seemed safe, and we never even thought about locking our doors unless we were going to be gone overnight. That day changed everything.

From the highway Hilley Road heads up to the northeast, passing our house about half a mile in. Past our place our only neighbor is Charlie's Creek Nursery, a tree farm on hundreds of acres. Beyond the nursery Hilley Road wanders through the hills, getting smaller and bumpier until it meets a county road about two miles from our house. Though the road was a shortcut to the boys' school, the route is not exactly short. We hardly ever used it and neither did the nursery employees. The killers did, though.

When the yellow school bus turned off the highway and onto Hilley Road, the rough pavement under the rumbling vehicle was like an alarm clock letting the boys know that they were finally home. The big bus rattled down the road for a minute before the driver, Mrs. Brown, brought it to a stop at the foot of our gravel driveway, which turns off the road like the right arm of a "Y." Mrs. Brown and the boys would have seen Johnny's black Ford F-150 parked in its usual spot near the road, in the shade of the old cedar that we used as an outdoor Christmas tree.

It was one of the hottest days of the year and, when Jeffrey and Tyler finally got home, it was after three in the afternoon. The temperature was well into the nineties and the humidity almost as high. As they got down out of the bus, the thick humidity slowed them down. Still, six-year-old Tyler kept up with his big brother as they walked up the driveway, which ran beside the road for about a hundred feet toward Johnny's truck.

Mrs. Brown maneuvered the big, yellow bus a little further down the road, to the far end of our property. She made a right turn, pulling the nose of the bus into a dirt track that actually circled the boundary of our land, up through the trees to the lawn area behind the house. Mrs. Brown backed up and made an oversized three-point turn to head the bus back toward the highway. Soon the bus was gone, though the disturbed dust lingered for a few moments.

The humidity hung on the boys as they lugged their bodies up the driveway, their sneakered feet crunching on the dirt. They headed toward the rear end of Johnny's truck, past the Johnny Quills that had long since died. Where the driveway reached the truck the gravel path turned up to the right, passing the play area where we had a swing set tucked in on the right-hand side. Johnny's mama had given the boys some of Johnny's childhood toys and a couple of his metal Tonka trucks still populated the sand box.

"Hey, Bubba," Tyler said, pointing down at the dirt driveway. "Look at that. You can see our four-wheel tracks!"

"Yeah," Jeffrey muttered. "I see."

The boys walked up toward the house, another hundred feet up from Johnny's truck. At the top of the driveway the gravel flattened out to a wide parking area with our house off to the left, parallel to the road. The house looked down over the lawn and a few trees.

The boys walked up to a small porch that protruded from the end of the house. Hopping up the steps. they stood on the small landing, pulled open the unlocked door, and walked into our dining area next to the kitchen.

The house was quiet and the air was stale, as if the air conditioner wasn't working properly. It was a hot afternoon, inside and out.

My husband worked nights—from eight in the evening until eight in the morning—so, when the boys came home from school, their daddy was often taking a nap. If they didn't see him outside, he was either sitting at his computer just beyond the kitchen or sleeping. Until that day, those were the only options. Quietly, Jeffrey and Tyler walked to the right into an alcove that led to their rooms on the far side of the house.

They used one bedroom as a playroom and the other as a sleeping room, which is where Jeffrey was headed. He put down his book bag and flopped onto the bottom bunk. "I'm gonna take a nap," he announced.

"Me too," Tyler said, following his big brother step-for-step. Tyler may or may not have needed sleep, but he wanted to do whatever Jeffrey did. Tyler dropped his backpack and squirmed onto the bunk next to Jeffrey.

At ten years old, Jeffrey watched out for Tyler. In fact, when Johnny started working nights, he told Jeffrey that he was the man of the house and he needed to take care of Tyler and me. And Jeffrey did. A very conscientious young man, he always acted responsibly and always seemed to think about what was right. It seemed like that was Jeffrey's nature, but I know we raised him that way. Johnny certainly did.

The boys didn't lie down for long. "I'm hungry," Jeffrey declared within a minute. "I'm gonna get me some cereal."

"Yeah!" Tyler said, hopping up and trailing him into the kitchen.

Just outside the bedroom hallway, Jeffrey turned to his right, opened the upper cupboard, and pulled out a box of Cocoa Pebbles, while Tyler walked across to the counter and reached up to get two bowls from the dish cupboard. Jeffrey joined him, putting the cereal on the counter and then shifting to his right to get the milk out of the fridge. As he pulled open the refrigerator door, something on the other side of the house caught his eye—too much light was coming through the laundry room, just beyond the living room.

Tyler watched his big brother, who closed the fridge and walked away into the big living room and toward the alcove that was near the middle of the far wall. That little hallway led to the master bedroom on the left and a utility room on the right. The utility room had cupboards, a washer and dryer, and then a door to the backyard. As Tyler watched Jeffrey walk through the living room, he understood why Jeffrey went over there. Sunlight was streaming into the alcove and it was obvious that the back door of the utility room was open to the backyard. Both boys knew that their father hated to have ladybugs in the house. They also knew that if Johnny found out that they had seen that open door and they didn't bother to close it, they'd be in trouble. Always well-behaved, Jeffrey went to close the door.

Our house was normally pretty well kept, but that day things were not where they belonged. As Jeffrey approached the alcove he noticed the gun cabinet, which stood against the wall separating the living room from the master bedroom. The cabinet still looked closed and locked, but a glass pane and part of the wooden frame were on the floor and a BB gun was sitting beside the cabinet. It didn't click in his mind that something might be wrong. Jeffrey assumed that Johnny had taken it apart to fix something. But then, Jeffrey noticed the area around our television. Usually all of our video tapes were put away, but as he walked by Jeffrey noticed that the tapes were pulled out and scattered around. It seemed to be in disarray, which was unusual for our house. Jeffrey did not understand.

Tyler watched as Jeffrey reached the alcove and turned to the right, toward the utility room. As Jeffrey turned into the laundry room, he suddenly understood. Johnny had not been working on little house projects. It was something much, much different. It was a nightmare.

Jeffrey's hands bolted to his face. He looked sick, panicked. "Daddy," he cried out. "Daddy!"

Get Tyler, he thought. *Get the phone! Call 911!*

Jeffrey retreated, walking to the back of the living room, toward the far corner where the couch sat under a window along the back wall.

Tyler didn't understand. *What is it?* he wondered, wanting to see it, too. He figured that the walls of the laundry room must have been covered with ladybugs. Since their daddy absolutely hated it when bugs got in the house, Tyler figured that Jeffrey had seen them all over the wall. *Oh, God, Daddy's gonna be mad,* he thought, walking across to the alcove. Tyler turned and looked at the utility room walls.

The walls were covered with blood. It looked as if the walls were painted red with blood. "I remember seeing blood everywhere," Tyler said later, somehow understanding that it was his father under all that blood. "I couldn't see his face," Tyler recalls. "It looked like a television crime scene, like a chalk-line drawing, where somebody got killed on the street and they drew a chalk-line shape in red. It was nothing but blood. All I saw was red and an outline of Daddy on the floor. That's all I saw—pure red—and the figure of him in the floor."

His father's body was lying at Tyler's feet. *What is this?* Tyler thought. At only six-years-old, he didn't know what he was seeing and didn't understand what was going on. He walked slowly to the living room and sat down on an ottoman.

Jeffrey's mind raced. He couldn't see anything but the image of his daddy, lying on his back in a wide pool of thick blood around his head and shoulders. His waist was across the threshold and his legs, in blood-soaked denim shorts, lay on the back porch with the open door up against his leg. Jeffrey saw his father's bare feet hanging out over the porch's top step. He saw one of his daddy's hands up on his chest near a broken steak knife, with serrated teeth and no handle that pointed up toward his chin.

Get Tyler, he thought. *Get away! Call 911!*

"Tyler!" he hissed. "Get over here!" He grabbed Tyler and yanked him to his side. They crouched in the corner near a table between the wall and the couch. Realizing that somebody had been in the house and might still be there—or could be waiting for them outside—Jeffrey wanted to get his back up against something so he could see everything. *If they're still here,*

13

he thought, they won't see or hear us.

Trying to figure out what had happened, Jeffrey suddenly understood quite a lot, especially for a ten-year-old boy. Although he went into a sort of shock, he kept his wits about him. Since he had never seen his daddy get hurt and not get back up, Jeffrey hoped that Johnny was okay, but he knew that he was probably dead. Though he was crying and scared out of his mind he listened to the house, knowing that someone had been inside and fearing that they were still there, or maybe outside, waiting for them. Terrified, Jeffrey reached for the phone.

He felt as if somebody was looking at him. He scanned the house. To his right, he looked again at the TV cabinet and saw that it was messed up, with the tape drawer hanging open and tapes lying on the floor. Through the alcove, the door to the master bedroom was open and the room was a mess. Things were thrown around and heaps of clothes were scattered everywhere. Just inside the door, the dresser drawers were pulled out and their contents were all torn up, and everything from on top of the dresser had been thrown off and scattered around the room. He looked again at the messed up gun cabinet near the alcove. With adrenaline pumping through his small body, his senses were heightened.

"Bubba," Tyler said.

"What?" Jeffrey asked.

"I know where they come in at."

"Where?"

"Right there," Tyler said, nodding toward the window. Right behind them, the living room window was broken.

Jeffrey continued to cry as he whispered to Tyler. "Stay with me and don't say nothing," he said, unaware that Tyler had looked into the utility room. "Stay down and be quiet, and don't move unless I tell you to move. They might still be in here."

Tyler didn't understand very much. Mostly, he felt upset because Jeffrey was upset. He was in six-year-old shock. All he could think was *What is this?* Nothing made sense to him. *What's going on?* Sobbing, Jeffrey dialed 911.

We had talked to our boys about what to do in case of an emergency. Johnny had taught them that if we had a fire in the house they should run out outside, get near our bedroom window, and "scream bloody murder and throw rocks at the window." Those were Johnny's words. I had taught the boys when and how to call 911. I told them that the call-taker would answer, "Abbeville County 911," and then she would ask, "Where is your emergency?"

But when Jeffrey called 911, the dispatcher did not say those words.

The phone clicked and the call-taker said, "Hello."

I was the 911 coordinator and often needed to call in to talk with my staff. The 911 Dispatch Center was a distance from our house, however, and it was a long-distance call for me to check in with the 911 telecommunicators. So when I needed to check in I often called 911 from my home phone, just as Jeffrey did that day.

Our 911 telecommunicators have three computer screens in front of them and, when a call comes in, initial information appears on one of those screens. That information includes the name, address, and phone number of the caller's residence. So before she answered the phone, my call-taker Christi Norton already knew that the call was coming from my house. She assumed that it was me, calling to touch base.

The call from my home came in at 3:25 p.m.

When Christi said, "Hello," Jeffrey didn't understand. Maybe he'd dialed wrong, he thought. Jeffrey didn't say anything. He hung up and dialed 911 again.

Again, Christi said "Hello." A telecommunicator for many years, Christi was in her late twenties, early thirties. She knew Johnny and she knew that

I had two sons.

"Is this 911?" Jeffrey asked.

"Yes," she said. "Do you have an emergency?"

"Is my mama there?" He asked.

Christi explained that I was at a doctor's appointment. "Do you need something?" she asked

"Something's wrong with my dad," he said.

"What do you mean 'something's wrong with him'?"

"He's bleeding," Jeffrey said.

"What do you mean he's bleeding?" she asked. "Where is he bleeding from? What's happened?"

"My daddy's bleeding," Jeffrey cried. "We came home and found him on the floor and there's blood everywhere."

"Is he conscious?" Christi asked as Jeffrey sobbed into the phone.

Jeffrey seemed confused about what 'conscious' meant, so Christi rephrased it. "Is he awake?"

"No," Jeffrey said.

"Is he breathing?"

"I'm not sure," he answered.

"We need to find out if he's breathing," Christi said. She could hear Tyler screaming in the background. Normally, if the caller is able, she would have assisted him in performing cardio-pulmonary resuscitation on the victim but Jeffrey was paralyzed with terror and, deep down, he also knew that it was too late.

"I can't," Jeffrey cried. "I can't go in there. There's too much blood."

Jeffrey told Tyler to be quiet and to sit still, and then he returned to the phone call. He mentioned the gun cabinet being messed up and said that a window was broken.

Christi was stressed, trying to determine whether Johnny was alive, and whether Jeffrey could help him. While she talked to Jeffrey, she could hear through her headset that her partner dispatched Emergency Medical

16

Services (EMS) and law enforcement. EMS was dispatched at 3:26 from Calhoun Falls, more than ten miles from our house.

"We need to find out if he's breathing," she suggested again, but Jeffrey was too upset. He could not do it. Unsure of whether Johnny was alive or not, Christi worried about the boys and their safety. Someone might have been in the house and the boys might have been in danger. And, as the conversation continued, it was sounding more and more like Johnny was already dead. Still, she tried her best to get Jeffrey to see whether Johnny was breathing.

"I can't go back in there," he repeated. "There's too much blood."

"We need to see if you can help him," she pressed. "I need you to go check on him."

"I'm not going back in there," Jeffrey insisted. Though he was praying that his daddy would make it, Jeffrey was beginning to lose hope.

Though he talked to Christi and answered her questions, he continued to be wracked with sobs. "My daddy's gone," Jeffrey wailed. "My daddy's gone!"

After accepting that Johnny was already dead, Christi's maternal instincts kicked in. As there was probably little that could help Johnny, she focused instead on trying to protect the boys and working to calm Jeffrey. As Christi's attention turned to Jeffrey, he seemed to panic more. She reassured him that help was coming to him—the deputies and rescue squad was coming to help him.

Every so often, Christi heard Jeffrey whispering to Tyler, telling him to stay quiet. Tyler didn't understand anything. He huddled next to Jeffrey, did what he was told, and sat there, looking around.

Again, Jeffrey mentioned the broken glass and the gun cabinet, and Christi reminded him not to touch anything and not to move.

"Help is coming," she said. "Help is coming."

CHAPTER 2

LADIES' MAN

I WAS TEN years old when I moved with my family from Farmington, Michigan to Lowndesville, South Carolina, and it seems as if I knew Johnny Hanna from then on. Friends from the beginning, we grew up together. All the kids in town knew each other and hung out together, and the same goes for me and Johnny even though he was eight years older than I was. Before they dammed up our river and turned it into a lake, we would walk down through Lowndesville and cross the river to a spot called the Pump House where we all went swimming. All those years I never developed feelings for him, but just thought of him as one of my friends.

Raised in Abbeville County, Johnny attended Calhoun Falls High in rural South Carolina. He grew large in stature—six-foot-one—and became a hefty teenager, earning the nickname "Fat Baby." He played football and was good at it. Football was a big deal in the South, in places like Lowndesville and Calhoun Falls, and that made Johnny something of a hero in our part of the world. He was the big man on campus; popular and gregarious, tall and strong. Larger than life, he lived as if the world turned around him because, at least when he was young, it seemed like it did. In his senior year, he received the "Mr. Flashes" award, which was a best all-around honor given to a senior who was something—popular, athletic, and well regarded.

When I was a teenager we hung out at places around town, including a really old store that sat by itself out on one of the country roads. The man who owned the place, who wasn't married and didn't have a family that we knew of, used to hang out with us, the young people. He'd cut up and entertain us by telling jokes or playing the guitar. We had a lot of fun times at his store.

As we got older, we started hanging out at a bar where we'd see our friends and other folks from around Iva, Lowndesville, and Calhoun Falls. During this time, Johnny and I became partying buddies, but not an official couple.

There was a rivalry among the guys from Iva and Lowndesville, a show of toughness. Everyone was aware of the rivalry including my sister, Sherri. Although Sherri was not the type of person who would hang out with the rough crowd, like I did, Sherri remembers hearing about the fist fights, which were set up like a showdown. If there was a fight, Johnny was sure to be there. He was tough and nobody got the better of him, ever.

By the time I was a senior in high school, I had developed a crush on Johnny. I was seventeen and he was twenty-five when I begged a friend of mine to ask him if he would go to the senior prom with me. When she asked him, he told her that he didn't think it was right because he was too old for me. Of course, I was hurt. I ended up going to my prom by myself, but I left early and came back to Lowndesville and met up with my lifelong friends Lee Davis and Michelle Yeargin. We were the three Lowndesville girls that hung out with the Lowndesville guys. Whatever mischief the guys were into, the three of us were usually close by. After my prom, we found Johnny and our buddies hanging out at the store. Johnny and I ended up talking well into the night about our lives in Lowndesville and our future with each other. Our relationship began to grow from there.

We weren't really "dating." We were kind of casually together for about a year before we started dating steadily. The problem, then, was that Johnny was very much in love with another woman. They had been together and then broke up, and that's when we started really dating, but things didn't stay steady between us. We'd get in an argument and break up, and he'd go back to her, and then they would break up and he'd come back to me. It went back and forth like that for a year.

Sherri didn't approve. She thought he was too old for me and that I was doing the chasing and he was doing the running. She'd tell me, "You know, you're gonna get what you deserve." The more studious and responsible daughter in our family, Sherri was the type of older sister who felt like she needed to "guide" me in the right direction.

Once, Johnny and I were going to meet another couple in Iva and we were all going to go out together. I got there and waited for Johnny with this other couple, but Johnny never showed up. The next day I called him repeatedly, but I didn't reach him until that night. He said he'd gone with some of his friends to hang out, but I didn't much care what his excuse was. We broke up.

Thinking back, I think our break-ups were all on him. Johnny would do things that would make me mad because he knew that I would say "Just forget it," and then he could back to that other girl. This happened many times. We'd break up and he'd go back to her, and then they would break up and he would come back to me. Not a bad deal, for him.

The way things were going, it seemed like something had to give. And, then, it did.

Johnny and I had been broken up for a week or so when I first found out that I was pregnant. When I told him, we agreed that we would try to make things work. We weren't going to get married, but we were going to be together. Still, we argued all the time and we were on-again, off-again.

Late in my pregnancy, Johnny and I found out I had preeclampsia, a dangerous pregnancy-induced high blood pressure. My doctor wanted to induce my labor on May 20, 1989. The night before I was admitted, Johnny and I went on a date. He told me that he didn't think it was a good idea for him to come to the hospital while my family was there. He and my mom didn't get along because she thought he should do more for me and the baby. Early the next morning, before my family arrived to take me to the hospital, Johnny told me to call him when it was okay for him to come up to see me.

I found out later that Johnny did come to the hospital while I was still in labor, asking the nurse if the baby had been born. When she said "no" he knew that everyone was still with me, so he left. During my pregnancy I felt that I was going to have a girl and had therefore prepared a girl's name. I had never given much thought about a boy's name. I was certainly surprised when Jeffrey was born! I didn't have a name for him so, on the first day of his life, the hospital referred to him as "Baby Boy Parnell." I then chose Charlton Jeffrey Parnell, deciding that we would call him Jeffrey.

Right after Jeffrey was born, Johnny's mom and dad came up to see us but I hadn't seen Johnny yet. I didn't see him until later that night, when the coast was clear. Johnny picked up Jeffrey for the first time. He was so scared and thought for sure that he was going to drop him. While I was nervous, I don't think I was as bad as Johnny. He wouldn't hold Jeffrey while he was standing up, but instead asked the nurse or me to hand Jeffrey to him while he was seated. He spent that night in the hospital chair beside me.

Our little family was working out pretty well, but it didn't last. When Jeffrey was about three months old, Johnny and I broke up again and, this time, we stayed broken up for a long time—a year and a half. It was bad.

My mama and dad were married to each other my entire life. That's the way I was raised and, in my eyes, when you marry you stay together. Now, I know that's not true; I know that things happen, and I understand that some people just don't belong together. Still, I did not want Jeffrey to call Johnny "Daddy" until Johnny comitted to fatherhood and we made it official through marriage. So, when Jeffrey started talking, one of his first words was "Da-da." Where he got that I don't know, because Johnny was not in the picture a whole lot. So, even though Jeffrey picked up "Da-da," I wouldn't let him call Johnny "Daddy." Johnny didn't see a problem with it, but, in my eyes, it wasn't right.

Even while Johnny and I were broken up, I knew that if I had gone to him and said, "Jeffrey needs diapers," he would have bought them or given me the money for them. But I was stubborn and I wanted to be able to support Jeffrey without being forced to go through Johnny. So I took Johnny to court to get child support. He wasn't speaking to me at the time because he was absolutely furious with me. Johnny was tight with his money and he didn't like the idea of being forced to spend money against his will.

We went to court and the judge told him he had to pay me something like ninety dollars a week in child support. Back then that was expensive, but the amount was based on Johnny's relatively substantial salary as an electrician.

Two or three days after our court appearance, Johnny's new girlfriend called me on the phone. "Since Johnny is having to pay child support to you," she announced, "we are going to pick Jeffrey up on Saturday and we are going to the lake."

"No, you're not," I said.

She ignored me and just kept going on about it. Finally, I hung up on her. About three minutes later, she called back.

"I'm telling you to have Jeffrey ready at seven o'clock," she said, "and we'll be by to pick him up."

I freaked out. My mom and dad were out of town so I called Mot and Stuart, my babysitter and her husband. I told them what Johnny's girlfriend had said and asked what I should do. Mot told me to bring Jeffrey to her house, because Johnny wouldn't go there to get him. That Friday, Mot had Jeffrey while I was at work and we agreed that I would pick him up later the next day on Saturday, after the threatened pick-up time.

On that Friday night, I got off work and went to the bar to have a few drinks with my friends. By the time Johnny and his girlfriend walked in, I'd had a little too much to drink. I was sitting at a table when she and I locked eyes. I hollered something stupid across the bar at her, and Johnny whipped his head around at me. "You just need to shut up," he said. That started it! I was hollering things at her until they left.

After that, she called three or four other times, threatening to come and get Jeffrey or telling me that I'd better have him ready to go. Years later, when Johnny and I were together and secure, I finally asked him if he had put her up to calling me all those times. He had no idea that she had even called me. "Why didn't you tell me that was going on?" he asked me.

"Because I thought you knew," I said. "I thought you were putting her up to it!"

Until Jeffrey was four-years-old, he and I lived in a cozy trailer on a wooded lot to the east of Lowndesville. Johnny would come and play with Jeffrey sometimes, but he wasn't consistent. Jeffrey remembers Johnny hooking up a little pedal go-cart to his four-wheeler and then riding it around the yard, pulling Jeffrey behind him. That was just like Johnny, but when Jeffrey was little, it wasn't enough. I was a single mom, dependent on Mot and my mama and dad for help. I hated to call Johnny when I needed something, but the trailer we lived in was not in great shape. There were no outdoor lights, no porch light, and half of the outlets didn't work. Even though Johnny was an electrician I called another electrician, a friend of ours named Tommy Brown. I asked him to come over to fix the lights and the outlets.

"Sheila," he said, "I will, but I think you need to call your baby's daddy and tell him that you need this stuff done."

"I'm not doing that," I said, flat out.

"Until you talk to him, I'm not coming."

I don't know how long it took, but I finally sucked up my pride and called Johnny. "Look," I said, "I need this stuff done, so I wanted to see if you could come over and fix it."

"Yeah," he said. "But you'll have to come pick me up."

Johnny'd had his driver's license taken away a few weeks earlier, so the next day I picked him up and he worked on some of the electrical problems in my house. Later that night, I drove him back home. It was the fall of 1991 and the Atlanta Braves were in the National League Championship Series, and we were really excited about baseball. There were more projects to do on the house so, when Johnny got off of work the next day, I picked him up again and he came to my house and worked on some more of the electrical problems, and then we watched the Braves' game. That night, I think Johnny and I both decided that we needed each other and that Jeffrey needed both of us. Johnny stayed over and he never left. That fall, Atlanta Braves took home the NLCS title and Johnny and I got back together.

The part of my life after Jeffrey was born until Johnny and I got back together was a rough time, but I think that both of us came to appreciate each other more. Finally, Johnny settled in and became a devoted and disciplined father.

The summer of 1992, Johnny worked four ten-hour shifts and had every Friday off, and I got off of work at two o'clock every day. One Friday when I got home, Johnny said, "Let's go apply for our marriage license." There was no "Will you marry me?" or getting down on one knee, just "Let's apply for our marriage license." Still, I said okay and we went. After we applied for the license, the judge said that we could return the following Monday to pick it up, but Johnny said that we'd be back the following Friday, his day off. I took that to mean that we would be getting married that next Friday.

When I went back to work on Monday I told all of my coworkers that I thought we were going to the courthouse to get married on Friday, after I got off work at two o'clock. So on Friday my friends at work threw me a bridal shower, just in case.

Later in the afternoon, Johnny saw me when I was bringing all the gifts into the house. "What's all this?" he said.

"They threw me a bridal shower today at work!"

"Who's getting married?" he asked.

"We are!"

"I didn't say we're getting married," he said

"You told that judge we would be back down there today..."

"Yeah, to go pick up the license."

I was flustered. "Well," I stammered, "I'll just give all these gifts back...

or something…" I was hurt and started to feel mad. I was determined that I would not marry him if he didn't really want to marry me.

"Heck no," he said. "Let's go! We're going to get married! Forget about a church wedding. We're going to the courthouse!" Johnny turned it around and, by the time we got to the judge on June 12, 1992, we were laughing. And then we were married. Truth be told, Johnny probably preferred going to the courthouse. I can't imagine him participating in a church wedding.

That week we'd had rain for almost a week, nonstop. It was raining everywhere around the Southeast. When Johnny asked me if there was someplace close-by where I wanted to go for our honeymoon, I told him it didn't matter to me. He said that, with the pouring down rain, he didn't want to go to Myrtle Beach and suggested we pick someplace where the rain wouldn't matter. We decided to go to Atlanta.

We didn't own suitcases, so we packed our clothes in trash bags and tossed them into the back of his beat up little Nissan truck. "Beat up" is a gross understatement. Johnny had ripped up that truck so bad that there was not a square inch on it that didn't have a dent. We arrived in Atlanta and pulled in to our hotel, which was verynice. Johnny saw that there was no self-parking, only valet. He said, "There's no way in heck I'm going in there and handing them a trash bag to carry up to our room!" So we left the hotel and went to the closest K-Mart to buy a suitcase. Standing in the pouring rain, we threw our clothes into the suitcase and then returned to the hotel to stay that Friday night.

The next morning, Johnny told me to call down to have the truck brought around while he got into the shower, so I called the valet. "This is Sheila Hanna," I said. "Can you please bring our Cadillac around?"

The guy said okay and asked for our tag number, and I hung up. I told Johnny that I was going to take the suitcase down and I headed downstairs. In a minute, the valet called back up to the room and Johnny answered the phone, unaware of what I'd said to the valet. "Mr. Hanna," he said, "the number that your wife gave me doesn't match up to a Cadillac. It matches a pick-up truck."

"What?" Johnny said. "I don't drive a Cadillac!"

In a few minutes, I was downstairs in the lobby. The valet brought the truck around just as Johnny got there. I didn't know that the valet had called and spoken to Johnny, but I did know that Johnny had an unhappy look on his face. We got into the truck, the guy put our K-Mart suitcase in the back and Johnny held his head down while he handed the valet a tip. Once we were driving down the road, Johnny finally said, "What did you tell them people when you called down there for the vehicle?"

I started laughing. "Why?" I asked. "How'd you know that I even said anything?"

Johnny told me the whole story. "That was embarrassing," he said. "I didn't even want to come down."

Truth be told, Johnny was proud of that truck, in a way. He had driven it forever, down dirt roads and through the brush. It was covered in dents, but it had almost two-hundred-thousand miles on it when he sold it.

Despite all our problems in the years before we got married, it all seemed to make us a stronger couple. Our marriage was surprisingly good. We were like a different couple and didn't have one argument in our first two years of married life. Our fighting completely stopped, and Johnny was an attentive and devoted husband and father.

"Are you going to let him call me Daddy?" Johnny asked me after we got married. Of course the answer was yes, and I changed Jeffrey's last name to Hanna. That name meant a great deal to Johnny, just as it means the world to his sons today. The Hanna name dates back several generations in our part of South Carolina, and many Hanna men—cousins, uncles, fathers, and grandfathers—are aware of the power of the name. Johnny epitomized the strong, disciplined, hardworking, and hard-living character of a Hanna man, and it was important to him to raise his sons in the tradition of that character. A loving father, he was also a strict man to whom reputation was paramount.

Johnny, Jeffrey, and I continued to live in the same trailer that I had been renting. Johnny and I decided quickly that we wanted to have another child, and Johnny hoped for another boy. To me, it truly didn't matter, though I did like to entertain the idea of having a little girl. Shortly after announcing my pregnancy, I left work and picked up Jeffrey at Mot's house. Arriving home, I noticed the screen door was wide open, which was unusual. I was cautious because, a year earlier when Jeffrey and I lived there alone, someone had broken into the house and stolen my television and all of our appliances. I reached for the doorknob and turned it. Taking one step into the house, I immediately realized that we had been robbed again. I grabbed Jeffrey and ran back to the car. When I got to Mot's house, we called the police and Johnny, who was at work. After that, Johnny decided the trailer was not a safe place to raise a family, so we set out looking for a new place.

CHAPTER 3

THE HANNA NAME

I N 1993, WHILE I was pregnant with Tyler, Johnny and I found the perfect place, a big lot that had plenty of trees on it. The land used to have an old home that sat up at the top of a rise away from the road, but the rickety wooden house had burned down and the owners put the property up for sale. That's when Johnny and I bought the place. Johnny had to get some trees removed so we could set the house where we wanted it, and then we moved in. This was the ideal place, just down the road from Mot and Stuart and about a mile from my parents and Johnny's.

The driveway ran along the west side of our land where the house was also set. Further back from the top of the driveway, Johnny built a rabbit box and we gave Jeffrey a white rabbit for his fourth birthday. I don't know how that rabbit got pregnant, but it did. Of course, when rabbits have babies they don't just have one or two, so Johnny had to build a divider for the cage. He would put the babies in one side and left the mama in the single cage alone. But sometimes, when Johnny was outside working in the yard by himself, he'd put Jeffrey in the cage for a short time with the white rabbit. As Jeffrey said, "That's Daddy's babysitting."

Late in my pregnancy, I had some pains and told Johnny that I thought I was in labor. Without hesitation he grabbed the suitcase, called Mot to tell her we were bringing Jeffrey, and then we were off to the hospital. We were there all night until four o'clock the next morning, when the doctor finally decided that it was false labor pains. The doctor said that since I'd had preeclampsia while I was pregnant with Jeffrey he would induce my labor three days later, on Thursday. But I didn't make it. On Wednesday evening, my true labor started. I knew that Johnny was tired from being up all night working, so I held off as long as I could. Finally, I had to tell him. "We got to get to the hospital," I said.

"I'm not going up there tonight for another dry run," he answered quickly. "I'll take you in the morning, when the doctor said to be there."

I wasn't sure if I wanted to laugh or kick his rear. Eventually, I convinced him that it was the real thing and we had to go. Hours later on May 27, 1993, we welcomed our second son, John Tyler Hanna. Johnny picked his name and we decided to call him Tyler.

Both of my little boys had blonde hair, though it darkened as they got older. Jeffrey's hair was curly, like Johnny's, but Johnny had dark brown hair. We all had curly hair, except for Tyler. Johnny hated his own curls and he hated that Jeffrey had the curls, too. He wanted to make sure that Tyler's hair didn't get curly. "Every time you look at Tyler," Johnny would tell me, "I want you to rub your hand down his head so his hair will grow straight." He really would do that. In one of the few videos that I still have, I can see Johnny rubbing down Tyler's hair. I suppose it worked, because today Tyler's hair is straight as a stick.

Jeffrey was the first grandchild in our family and, when he was just a little guy, my cousin started calling my brother "Uncle Bubba." Everyone in the family, even my sister's kids, started calling him Uncle Bubba. Then, a bit later, my uncle gave Jeffrey a dog and, when we asked him what to name the dog, he suggested "Bubba." Then, when Tyler started talking, I was calling Jeffrey "Bubba" and Tyler picked it up, so then we had Uncle Bubba, the dog Bubba, and our son, Bubba. Everything was Bubba except Johnny, whose nickname was "Fat Baby." Tyler looked so much like Johnny that he inherited the name and, even now, some people in Lowndesville refer to Tyler as "Fat Baby Junior."

With Johnny's great sense of family pride, he paid a lot of attention to his reputation and worked hard toward discipline. A hardworking man who emphasized self-control and personal strength, he was a strict father who took care of business. If he told the boys to do something, that meant that he wanted it done now and they knew that they'd better do it quickly. My boys knew that they had to do what they were told to do and that, if they didn't, they'd be in trouble with Johnny. If Johnny found out that something had gone wrong with the boys, he wasn't one to simply fix it. He'd want to know what happened, what the boys were up to, and what had caused the problem. Then he'd straighten it out. His parenting skills were very different from my own. As long as they listened to him and did what they were supposed to do, everything went fine. While I was more likely to give in, Johnny didn't let the boys push the limits. Most of the time, they didn't.

Being so young, Jeffrey still made little mistakes and he grew up thinking that his daddy was very strict. At the same time, Johnny was a better disciplinarian than I was. For one thing he was super strong and his punishment hurt. Jeffrey said that Johnny would give him a whipping to make sure he learned something, and that I would give a spanking as if I had to look like I was punishing him. And even though Jeffrey knows that Johnny was much more strict than some parents, he knew right from wrong and made a serious effort to stay out of trouble.

In another sense, Johnny was a very sweet daddy. He was more likely to give them treats than I was. For example, every week I would take the boys up to Anderson to do our major shopping and, every time before we'd leave, Johnny would ask Jeffrey and Tyler if they needed some money. They knew that, if they asked Johnny, he might give them some. Of course, they also knew that if they asked and Johnny said no, it was never going to happen.

From the time when the boys were young, we taught them good manners.

They always addressed adults as "Sir" or "Ma'am" and said "Please," "Thank you," and "You're welcome." We were more casual around the house but whenever the boys were in public, like when talking to a server at a restaurant or other adults, we thought it was important.

Johnny also told them that young men don't go out to other people's homes or businesses with their shirttails out of their pants, so, unless we were around the house, my boys always had their shirttails tucked in and their undershirt never showed. At least, that's true when they were away from home. Around the house was another story.

Tyler remembers one time when Johnny woke the boys up early one morning and got them outside. All they had on was socks and their underwear—not boxers, but tighty-whiteys. All three of them came outside and Johnny had three or four squirrels up in the tree and he brought the boys out there and shot the squirrels. "That's a real redneck!" says Tyler. "It was crazy, but we ate 'em." An avid deer hunter, Johnny hunted anything that moved and ate every bit of it. He'd even quit smoking before hunting season because, if he didn't come home with a buck, he figured his Marlboro Lights were to blame.

One year, a few weeks into hunting season, Johnny had not succeeded in killing a single deer yet and was very disgruntled about it. As a joke, I put a note in his lunch box with a poem that I'd made up: "Roses are red, violets are blue, the deer are in the woods, hiding from you." He laughed about it, and then kept that note in his important papers.

Johnny was the kind of daddy who was busy with his sons almost all the time. Whenever the boys were at home, they'd be doing things around our place with Johnny. For the most part, their life was like Johnny's—they'd stay busy together, enjoying the outdoors and taking care of chores, and then he'd go to work and they'd go to school. Johnny and I helped Jeffrey with his homework as much as we could. I helped him to learn spelling by thinking up objects to represent the letters, and when Jeffrey had to learn all the planets, I made up a sentence using the first letter of each planet. Jeffrey still remembers it: "My very easy mother just sat under new possums!"

One year, Jeffrey had to do a science project which Johnny made it for him—a piece of plywood with a light bulb and a dimmer knob. The whole point of it was to show how much power is used by different facilities—a power plant, a school, a house. When Jeffrey tried and failed to make his own, Johnny allowed him to use the one he'd made as an example.

Super Nintendo was popular then and we played it for a while every night. Johnny didn't want the boys playing video games or watching TV during the daytime unless the weather was bad. During the daytime, he wouldn't let the boys stay inside at all. If Johnny was outside, he wanted the boys outside—and he was always outside. Johnny's theory was that if you stay inside, you become lazy. He believed that being outdoors rejuvenates a person's mind and body. Although they did chores and took care of the yard and the land, Johnny would also constantly play with the boys. They'd ride ATVs together at least once or twice every day, skipping around in the dirt. Jeffrey drove Johnny's four-wheeler until he got his own for Christmas when he was six. When they weren't on their four-wheelers, the three of them would ride their bikes up and down our road and they'd plant crops, go fishing, repair equipment, and build things. Some people see these kinds of activities as chores but, to Johnny and my boys, this was just life.

They always enjoyed baseball. When he was young Jeffrey was a small kid, so we were happy that he preferred baseball over something high contact like football. Jeffrey played every year, starting at age five, and Johnny was always his coach. So every year before the season started, Johnny would take Jeffrey out to start getting ready for baseball. Johnny taught Jeffrey how to hold the ball and how to throw, and he would pitch to Jeffrey, who learned how to hit the ball back to him. They played catch out in front of the house on our lawn, by an old tree where Johnny taught Jeffrey left from right. Jeffrey would throw the ball to one side or the other of the tree, and he'd have to tell Johnny where the ball went so he could go get it. Even though Johnny knew where it was, he wanted Jeffrey to describe it, left or right, but Jeffrey would point and say, "It went on that side of the tree." Johnny kept on asking, "You going to tell me left or right?" Jeffrey guessed until he got it right but, from then on, he remembered which was which.

One year, we gave the boys a race car track for Christmas. Johnny and I stayed up all night putting it together and then we played with it until almost six in the morning. Finally, we got into bed and then a couple of minutes later the boys came in to wake us up for Christmas morning. We hadn't even fallen asleep yet. Johnny's birthday was on Christmas Day, so our routine was that Johnny would play with the boys and their new toys while I cooked breakfast for our entire family, who came over to celebrate Johnny's birthday. Since it was Johnny's birthday, Christmas was a very special holiday in our family.

When the boys were about eight and four, Johnny took them to the movies to see George of the Jungle. After that, the boys found a long vine that went up one of the big trees near the house. They grabbed onto it and swung back and forth, pretending they were George and swinging out over our big sandbox, which was populated with toys. Finally, the boys broke the vine. Johnny's mama, Barbara, had saved a lot of Johnny's toys from when he was kid, like the Tonka truck. Johnny had played with it through his whole childhood and it was still in one piece, so Barbara gave it to Jeffrey and Tyler. She was going to give them the rest of his toys when they got older, but tragedies intervened. Johnny's father still has all of those old toys.

The play area was alongside our driveway, which was lined with Johnny Quills, little yellow flowers like buttercups that bloom in the spring. They popped up at the side of our property, so we dug them up and planted them all along our driveway until the whole area was overflowing in Johnny Quills. Covered with the happy yellow blossoms, our yard was very pretty during the springtime.

Our property was wide along the road and we had a dirt track at the other end that ran up to the backyard. Behind our house, our land went down a forested hill to a creek that fed the lake, just east of Lowndesville. The creek and lake were not far from our place and Johnny and the boys would often go fishing down there.

Along the front of our house we had a deck off the living room and the front of the deck was lined with a wooden flower bed. It had metal posts with sweet sayings perched on top. Near the deck, in the front yard, we had planted a few pear trees but I still joke that we must have been cross-eyed on the day we planted those trees because they're all crooked.

Johnny was home by himself one day when he decided to put a deer stand up in a tree for Jeffrey. He was up in the tree when his ladder fell and he couldn't get down. He was stuck up there. Johnny heard a truck and saw that the guy who owned the nursery nearby was driving down the road with his window down, so Johnny started hollering, calling the guy's name. The guy finally heard, stopped his truck, and listened. "Where are you?" he said. Johnny kept hollering and, finally, the guy spotted his striped shirt, high up in the tree.

We had one big tree down in front of the house that looked like a Christmas tree, so we decorated it every year. Over the years, we did cut a few Christmas trees to use inside the house, which was nice. Since the whole place had been covered with a forest of pine and oak, Johnny cleared a lot of the land in front of the house. He kept plowing and working to prepare a field, down near the dirt track. As he cleared trees, Johnny accumulated a big pile of wood and then, after we'd lived there for about four years, he finally burned it all.

We worked so hard to clear up the place. With more than eleven acres, Johnny worked endlessly to get rid of the stumps that had been left, and then we planted the flowers, put up a hammock in the backyard, and fixed up a nice half-moon deck and swimming pool.

Johnny always kept a nice assortment of crops growing in the vegetable garden. He grew anything and everything—corn, tomatoes, cucumbers, peas. He tried to grow pumpkins and watermelons a couple of times, and other stuff that he would just grow just to see if he could, but the most successful crops were all the vegetables that I could can. Then he would go hunting and we would use the deer meat and whatever vegetables that we harvested out of the garden to make stews.

I didn't go in the garden as much as Johnny because I am terrified of snakes and we had our share of little green snakes on our land. So one year, when it came time to pick the vegetables, I drove the four-wheeler through the rows—with my feet up off the ground and away from the snakes—pulling the boys in the wagon behind me so they could pick the crops.

Johnny was very particular about the house, the yard, and the land, and it was important to him to keep it all in good shape. He was the kind of guy who always puttered around the house, and was always making improvements. It got to the point that he didn't want me to even cut the grass because I didn't know how to do it his way. We had our place nicely fixed up and we were proud of what we had. It was a beautiful spread, as green as can be, and our life was good.

Still, you worry about things. I used to worry about Johnny working our land on the tractor. The yard behind the house slopes down and I used to see Johnny on the tractor back there, cutting grass or working the land, and I worried about the tractor flipping over. "One day," I used to say, "that thing is going to turn over with you on it!"

As meticulous as he was about our property, he was just as disciplined as a father. He taught our boys about responsibility, especially Jeffrey, because he was old enough to learn. Jeffrey had a good time, riding on the four-wheeler, playing, riding bikes, fishing, and living life. But, when he misbehaved, Johnny straightened him out with a spanking—called a whipping in our neck of the woods.

One time, I was at work and Jeffrey was with the babysitter, Mot. She had sat for me ever since Jeffrey was a baby, and she was like another grandmother to my sons. Mot and Stuart lived in a big house at the corner where the bus turned off the highway onto Hilley Road. Jeffrey was wearing some blue-jean cut-off shorts that had a string hanging off them, and he got the bright idea to burn off that string. Of course, he set his shorts on fire and burned his leg. Mot got the fire out and then, when Johnny and I found out, Jeffrey got a whipping for setting himself on fire. According to Jeffrey, the spanking hurt more than the fire did.

When Jeffrey was really young he picked up the habit of using cuss words and, to punish him, we would make him take a sip of buttermilk. One day, at Mot's house, Jeffrey ordered Mot to turn on the air conditioner.

"I'm not turning the air conditioner on," Mot answered.

"I'm hot," Jeffrey persisted. "Turn the air conditioner on."

"I said I was not turning it on," Mot snapped back.

"Mot," Jeffrey said, "turn the damn air conditioner on!"

Needless to say, Jeffrey got a taste of buttermilk.

Sometime later, Jeffrey met me at Mot's door and told me that Mot's husband, Stuart, had been saying "bad words."

"Why?" I asked.

"I didn't hear him," Jeffrey said. "But Mot is making him drink buttermilk!" Stuart just enjoyed a glass of buttermilk with his lunch.

One day, Johnny was having the boys pick up rocks in the backyard and Jeffrey got tired of it and quit helping. That didn't fly well with Johnny, who fussed at Jeffrey to get back to picking up rocks.

"So," Jeffrey said, seriously, "you want me to pick up sticks too?"

Johnny assumed that Jeffrey was being a smart-aleck and his beady eyes shot right through Jeffrey, who instantly knew he'd better get back to picking up rocks.

If the boys said something sassy, Johnny and I used to say, "You better watch your mouth." We didn't know it but Jeffrey interpreted that literally for a long time. One day, I said that to Jeffrey and he said, "But, Mama, I can't see my mouth." At first, I thought he was being smart but he was dead serious.

Jeffrey remembers one time when he got a whipping and really understood the reason. In second grade, he had gotten into a fight. The other boy started it and the two only hit each other a couple times before it ended, but Jeffrey came home with a pair of red marks on his legs. Johnny told him that he'd better not be going to school starting fights and, if he did get into a fight, that he'd better have more scratches and bruises on his knuckles than anywhere else on his body. Jeffrey said that he tried not to get into the fight because he didn't want to get in trouble. Johnny said that he'd be in trouble either way and, besides, if he got beat up in the fight then he'd get two whippings—the first being the fight and the second being the spanking from Johnny for losing.

Though Johnny was strictly the dad around the boys, he'd had his wild days and his share of fights. People knew that he would never let anyone push him around. That was a responsibility that Johnny passed on to his sons, especially Jeffrey. He wanted the boys to know that they should never back down, but should stand up for what they think is right. Jeffrey passed this along to Tyler. I believe that it was important to Johnny to teach the boys to give one hundred percent, and don't think about losing in anything. We did not condone fighting, but I think that this came up in their father-son talks, when Johnny showed his sons his pride.

When Jeffrey was nine, he was playing baseball and practicing for the All-Stars in July. A good baseball player in multiple positions, Jeffrey made the All-Star team every year. But that year it was terribly hot, probably over one hundred degrees outside, and Jeffrey passed out in the outfield. He woke up as Johnny was coming to get him and talking to him, but Jeffrey had blacked out and couldn't see his Daddy. Johnny grabbed Jeffrey's arm and started walking him to the dugout. "Walk!" Johnny said. "Stand up. You got to walk. You got to walk!"

But Jeffrey couldn't walk. As he woke up, Johnny took off Jeffrey's shirt and wet his neck, and Jeffrey finally came to. By the time they got home and Johnny told me what had happened, he was concerned about Jeffrey but, in an effort to show Jeffrey toughness, he gave him a hard time. "Your son passed out today," Johnny would say. "And he was the only one that passed out." It was in fun, but Johnny felt that Jeffrey passed out because he wasn't used to the heat, so he also wanted to tell Jeffrey to get stronger. This would be only one of his strategies of teaching the boys a lesson.

Later that summer, on a very hot afternoon, Johnny wanted the boys to go outside and play basketball but Jeffrey wanted to take a nap. Johnny threw it back at Jeffrey that if he didn't get outside and get used to the weather, he'd keep passing out. As much as Johnny pushed that, Jeffrey didn't go outside. Johnny got upset. He wanted the boys to make their own mistakes and learn from them. After that, he made Jeffrey hydrate more or eat a candy bar before it was time to go outside, so that he'd be able to tolerate the heat.

It was important to Johnny that his sons be like him; disciplined and responsible, strong and tough. Tyler was young yet, but Jeffrey worked hard at learning the lessons that Johnny tried to teach him. By example, Johnny taught the boys to take care of their family and friends. If anyone called on Johnny to help them, he would. My sister still calls her Christmas lights "Johnny's lights," because he fixed them up for her two Christmases before he was killed.

"I could not get my lights to work," Sherri said, "and they didn't sell these lights anymore." They were the kind that could play music with the lights blinking along to the tune. "Please come help me," Sherri told Johnny. "These are my favorite lights." He worked on them for hours, rewiring the lights and fixing them so the music worked. "Johnny was tough and rough," Sherri said. "He could be hard sometimes, but he'd give you the shirt off his back, whatever he needed to do to help."

By example, Johnny also taught our boys courage. Jeffrey always believed—and still does—that the only difference between his dad and Superman was that his dad couldn't fly. Johnny set a great example of strength and self-reliance, and, as the boys grew older, they emulated that. But, when they were young, they always believed that Johnny would save them, no matter what happened.

When Jeffrey was young, he'd get spooked around the house, like any child might. If he was alone in the living room and had to go to the trash can, he would run to the trash can and back to the living room, without turning on a light or slowing down for anything. If he heard a noise, he'd make a straight sprint to his room, scared that a monster was going to get him in the dark. When he was a little boy and still taking baths, then heard a scary noise, he would think about what to do if a bad guy came after him. Jeffrey told himself that if a murderer came in to kill him, he would talk to the guy long enough for his dad to come and save him. He always told himself that he could do that.

Maybe we thought about things like that because Johnny worked nights and I was home alone with the boys so much of the time. One night, I got really scared. Johnny was working, as usual, and it was about eleven o'clock. I was in our bedroom alone and saw a car pull up in front of the house. It was out on the road, not in the driveway, but it pulled up directly in front of the house, turned off its headlights, and set on its parking lights. I've never shot a gun but I was sitting there thinking about my boys in their beds and thought, Okay, I'd better get a gun. I stood in the dark house, peering through a window at the truck, and then I went to the living room, sat on the couch, and picked up the phone.

I called Johnny at work, at West Point Stevens textile mill in Calhoun Falls.

"There's a truck parked right in front of our house," I said, "with nothing but its parking light on!"

"Alright," he said. "I'll be there in a minute."

"Tell me," I said. "How do you load these guns?"

"Sheila, don't mess with it," he said. "You put the gun up."

I didn't just have one gun. I had two or three of them lying out on the couch.

In a bit, the truck took off. Not five minutes later, Johnny pulled up the driveway. I walked out the side door as he got to the parking area and I told him that the truck went on down the road, so Johnny took off down the road, too. He was gone at least thirty minutes. I was thinking the worst. I figured that they got him and I was fixing to call the police but just then, Johnny pulled his truck back into the driveway.

"Dang," Johnny said when he walked back into the house. "You had me chasing my uncle down the road! He was out trying to find his coon dogs." Of course, I felt dumb for letting my imagination get away from me.

Still, those experiences serve a purpose, helping us to prepare ourselves for what we would do, if… By the same token, we always tried to teach our boys—especially Jeffrey—what to do in case something did happen. Get Tyler. Call 911. Obviously, we weren't expecting something like Johnny's murder, but, still, we prepared him for the unexpected. It seems ironic now.

While working at 911 I had endured some heart-wrenching emergency calls, some of which would have been much smoother if the person calling in knew what to expect. With this in mind, I wanted to make sure that Johnny and the boys knew what to expect if they ever had to call 911. I told them, when you call 911 the call-taker is going to ask for your address. I remember Johnny asking, "Why would they ask for the address if it comes up on the computer screen?" I explained that they needed to verify that the information is correct and that the caller's address is where the emergency is. I also explained that they would ask questions but while they do so, they are dispatching help, so don't get frustrated thinking that help is not on the way. We even practiced calling 911, with the boys and Johnny playing the callers and me playing the call-taker. And, sometimes, the boys would ask me to tell them about some of my 911 calls.

A big and strong man, Johnny was very protective. Actually, he was protective of us, of his name, and of himself. He was the kind of man who didn't like to even think that he was being run over. If he felt like he was being taken advantage of, he would call a halt to it without a second thought. It was his nature to stand up for his family and for himself.

Before Tyler had started kindergarten, Jeffrey's school bus came to our driveway at five-thirty in the morning. Since he didn't have to be to school until eight, five-thirty was really early for a bus but Jeffrey and a classmate, Joy Compton, lived the farthest away from school so they were always the first to get on and the last to get off. One day we'd all overslept, only just waking up when the bus arrived. Jeffrey wasn't ready for school, so Johnny rolled out of bed and walked outside, down the driveway and out to the bus. Shaking off the cobwebs of sleep, he climbed up into the bus and told the driver that it didn't make any sense to be coming by at five-thirty in the morning. They need to fix it, he told her. Johnny stood out there for ten minutes, waiting for Jeffrey to get ready. Of course, Jeffrey was mortified but, at the same time, he was proud that his daddy stood up to them like that, and that he held the bus so that Jeffrey wouldn't be late to school. About a week later, the bus schedule changed.

Johnny didn't have as many opportunities to influence Tyler, who was only six-years-old when his daddy died, but Johnny did all he could in a short time, teaching his younger son about being a Hanna man. Tyler always shadowed Jeffrey, learning as much from him as he did from his daddy, but Johnny made a strong impression on Tyler, too.

CHAPTER 4

THE LAST SUMMER

JOHNNY OFTEN TOOK the boys out hunting and shooting guns. He had several guns—shotguns, .22s, and larger rifles. At five years old, Tyler was scared of shotguns and much preferred to use his BB gun. Sometimes, Johnny and the boys would even take target practice off the front porch. Other times, we'd set up cans on a log for Tyler to shoot, while Johnny and Jeffrey would shoot targets over the pasture.

The first time Tyler ever shot a shotgun, he and Johnny had just returned from squirrel hunting and Tyler had been aggravating Johnny all day about wanting to shoot his gun. On and on, Tyler kept saying that he wanted to shoot his daddy's gun. So they finally came back to the house and Johnny was going to make Tyler shoot his gun. Tyler sat in Johnny's lap and Johnny held the shotgun, resting it back against Tyler's shoulder.

Looking back, Tyler thought his daddy was bluffing, trying to get him to stop aggravating him about shooting that gun. "It's gonna hurt you," Johnny warned the boy. Knowing how Tyler was iffy about pulling triggers on anything—even his own BB gun—Johnny figured Tyler would never pull the trigger on that shotgun, so he was about to set the gun down. Just as he did, Tyler pulled the trigger. The kick knocked both of them back, even

Johnny! "I don't want to shoot no guns no more!" said Tyler. After that, Tyler mostly stuck to shooting the bow and arrow or BB gun when he went shooting with Johnny.

When Jeffrey was ten and Tyler was six, their last summer with their daddy, Johnny decided to have the boys stay home with him during their summer vacation rather than having them go to Mot's every day as we'd always done. The boys were old enough that Johnny could manage his night shift, sleep in the morning, and deal with the boys, too. He had a good time with them for the summer and it turned out to be an incredible blessing that they had the time together.

Johnny worked third shift, from eight in the evening until eight in the morning. Before he left for work at night he'd say, "See you cats in the sandbox." When he had a moment with Jeffrey, he'd remind him to take care of Tyler and me when he was gone. "You've got to be the man of the house," he would often say.

In the mornings, Johnny would usually come home and sleep for a while before getting busy with the boys. On his last workday of each week, he'd stay up after work to try to be on a normal sleep schedule for the weekend. So, for the most part, when the boys were up, Johnny was up. And, as usual, they would all be outside doing activities.

Late in the afternoons, the boys and Johnny would go inside and relax. Jeffrey and Tyler watched Cartoon Network while Johnny would get on the computer and play solitaire. Then, when I got home from work we'd have dinner before Johnny went to work and then I would often play Nintendo with the boys. I loved to play, and Jeffrey and I did that a lot.

Other than those times, my boys have very few memories of being inside. Jeffrey liked to watch fake-professional wrestling, which Johnny also liked, and they did that now and then. One year, they were in a serious jam because wrestling was going to be on during the same time as the Super Bowl. Our house wasn't wired for cable in multiple rooms, so it was a problem. For Johnny, the Super Bowl took precedence and that meant that Jeffrey wasn't going to be able to watch wrestling. But Johnny the electrician—and Daddy the hero—came up with a solution. He ran a wire into Jeffrey's bedroom and set him up to watch wrestling while Johnny watched the Super Bowl in the living room. Whenever Jeffrey wanted to switch from the football game to the wrestling match, he would hit the page button on the phone, which would ring in the living room so Johnny knew to hit the remote to switch Jeffrey's TV back and forth.

There were a few special shows like that but, otherwise, Johnny turned off all the movie channels during the summertime. Since they were costly and he didn't want the boys inside anyway, he would just get rid of those channels for a few months. So he and the boys were outside almost all of the time, playing in the woods, riding their four-wheelers, building me a clothesline, or working in the garden. We even bought a trampoline—the scary kind, without walls—and an above-ground pool. And Johnny paid the boys to catch ladybugs, which were a big problem that year. He gave them a nickel for every ladybug they collected in a jar. That whole summer the boys had plenty to do, and Johnny was able to do it with them, thank God.

We took a family vacation to Myrtle Beach that summer, our last vacation as a family. Johnny was not big on spontaneous trips so I found a cheap room because he didn't like to spend money, either. We booked it and planned the trip. Unfortunately when we showed up, the room had holes in the walls. Johnny said, "We are not staying here!" Johnny demanded that the hotel credit his account for the deposit. After doing so, we moved to another hotel.

We had so much fun on that trip and the boys were ecstatic when Johnny helped them build their sandcastle on the beach. One day they went to the beach early in the morning to hunt for sharks' teeth. They found three perfect sharks' teeth, which I now have displayed in a picture frame. I am so thankful that we had that trip together and for those memories.

The other thing that happened that summer was deeply personal to our family, and very important to Johnny. In the end, it became the most important thing to me, too. Johnny was saved.

My family hadn't been very religious when I was growing up, but Johnny's family was. His mama and father went to church every Sunday and Johnny grew up with religion, so he made a rule that we would raise our children with a church life. Every other weekend, when Johnny was off work, we attended church as a family and I took the boys by myself whenever I could. But, still, we'd gotten off to a rocky start and none of us had ever been baptized.

Even though Johnny wanted the boys raised in the church, he didn't want religion to be forced on him and he didn't want to be forced to be baptized or saved. He felt that this should be a personal decision between himself and God. I felt like I had to tip-toe around the issue, like I had to be careful about what I said about my faith, because, for me, it was changing.

Johnny and I had been going to church and I remember telling him so many times that I was ready to walk the aisle. "I'm going to walk the aisle today," I would say. "I'm going to walk the aisle today." But I couldn't ever get my body to go down there.

Walking the aisle happens every Sunday at church. The preacher always extends the invitation, which can be a couple of things. Some people will walk the aisle to say the Sinner's Prayer and be saved. Some people will walk down to ask to be accepted as a member of the church, and others will just walk to ask the preacher to pray for them, which he will do right then and there.

I got saved during Vacation Bible School. In our church—Southern Baptist—a person is saved when he or she acknowledges being a sinner. When I admit to my church that I am a sinner and profess my belief that Jesus Christ died on the cross for my sins, I am saved. It's not exactly a commitment, but a process of growth and acknowledgement. When I was saved I was asked, "Do you believe Jesus Christ died on the cross for your sins?" To be saved, this is the important element that we must believe in order to receive the sacrificial gift Christ gave to us.

"Yes," I answered. I recited "The Sinner's Prayer," stating that I am a sinner and asking the Lord for forgiveness. That's the prayer, and that was my salvation.

Afterward, the boys and I had come home and Johnny was outside, cooking fish. Since I had been saved, I was really excited and I wanted to share the news with him. "Guess what?" I said.

"What?" he said.

"I got saved tonight!"

"You did?"

"Are you not excited?"

"I'm excited for you," he said.

A day later, I couldn't resist. "I really wish you would talk to this preacher," I said.

"I will," he said. "In my own time. Don't push me"

"I wouldn't wait too long," I said. It was in a warning tone, though casual, because I didn't want to pressure him. I knew that if I did, it would backfire.

I wanted Johnny to talk to the preacher for two reasons. First, I wanted him to be saved. The second reason was because there was a new preacher at our church and I thought Johnny might be open up to him. What I didn't know was that Johnny's father, Marshall, was talking to Preacher Griggs about coming to our house to talk to Johnny. The preacher came to me one Sunday after church and said, "Sheila, I really feel like I need to talk to Johnny."

"Yeah," I said. "I want you to but, I'm telling you, you need to be really careful." I warned him about one specific incident when Johnny and I were dating and he still lived with his parents. I was at their house when the preacher at the church at that time came over and pushed himself on Johnny. Johnny got really mad and walked out, leaving the preacher and everybody sitting there. I didn't want that to happen again.

Soon after the preacher spoke to me, Johnny asked me to invite Preacher Griggs over for dinner so he could talk to him. When the preacher came to our house to talk to Johnny, the boys and I went outside to give them privacy. I didn't know what Johnny would do. They finished talking and the preacher left, but Johnny didn't share anything with me. I had no idea what he felt. After a few days, I figured that nothing had happened between Johnny and the preacher.

All of a sudden in late June, 1999, Johnny took the boys and walked the aisle. He never forewarned me and I didn't know until that moment that he was going to walk down. Jeffrey and Tyler walked by his side, one at each hand, and they walked to the front of the church. As Preacher Griggs reached out to shake Johnny's hand and pray, Johnny told him, "Wait, just a minute." Johnny proceeded with the boys down to the altar, where he knelt between them. The boys followed him, all three bowing their heads while I watched from the pew. When he talks about Johnny today, Preacher Griggs often refers to this day when Johnny knelt and prayed with the boys.

In July Johnny, Jeffrey, and I were baptized. Our preacher and members of our church gathered at the shore of the lake and then the preacher baptized a couple of other people. Johnny helped out, ushering people out of the water before it was our turn. The preacher prayed over each of us and announced that we were accepted into the church. As he spoke over Jeffrey, Johnny patted his son on the shoulder.

A month later, Johnny was gone. I thank God that I know where he is.

CHAPTER 5

WE DIDN'T KNOW THEY WERE PRAYING FOR US

O N THURSDAY, AUGUST 5, Johnny smiled as the boys and I left the house. "See you cats in the sandbox," he said.

Though Johnny was the assistant coach for Tyler and Jeffrey's baseball team, he couldn't come with us to the awards dinner that night. He had to go to work, so I took the boys to the dinner by myself. It wasn't supposed to be a big deal, but Johnny missed out when Jeffrey received a special award for the season that Johnny didn't know he was getting.

The boys and I left the banquet dinner at about 6:30. The first day of school was the next day and we needed to squeeze in some back-to-school shopping for the boys' school clothes and supplies. We decided to take care of that. But first, I needed to stop by our house to get Johnny's credit card. I waited in the car while Jeffrey ran in for me.

"What're you doing here?" Johnny asked Jeffrey.

"We're going back-to-school shopping," Jeffrey said. "Mama needs your credit card."

"Okay," Johnny said, walking to retrieve his wallet while his son followed. "How was the dinner?"

"Good," Jeffrey said, following his daddy. "Did you know I got the Best

All-Around award?"

"You did?" Johnny was surprised.

"You didn't know?" Jeffrey asked.

"No," Johnny smiled. "I'm proud of you, son."

"Thanks, Daddy."

Johnny gave Jeffrey the credit card. "Tell Mama not to spend a lot of money just because she has my card," he said. "And don't forget, while I'm at work you're the man of the house. Take care of Mama and Tyler."

"I will, Daddy," Jeffrey said. "See you tomorrow!"

That was the last time Jeffrey saw his father alive.

Jeffrey got back in the car, handed me the card, and relayed the message about not spending too much. We drove to the highway and turned north, heading up to the town of Anderson, about twenty miles north of Lowndesville.

After about ten minutes, I noticed a cloud in the shape of someone down on his knees, praying. "Look, boys!" I said, pointing to the cloud. "God is sending someone a message."

I didn't know then that the message was for us.

We were still out when Johnny left for his job as a night-shift electrician. By the time we got home that night, Johnny was gone.

I woke up early the next morning, the first day of school at Diamond Hill Elementary for Jeffrey and Tyler. Jeffrey was starting fifth grade and Tyler was starting first grade. The boys were good about getting themselves ready for school, dressing in simple blue jeans and T-shirts. Normally, they would take the school bus to and from school but, since it was the first day of the new year, I drove them to school that day and they would take the bus home. The boys and I left the house a few minutes after 7:30 and I was back home before 8:00, before Johnny got home from work.

Since I had a doctor's appointment in the late morning, I didn't go to work that day. That was helpful because we planned to host a back-to-school pool party that night. It would be one last blast of summer fun, with hot dogs, swimming, and all the young people from our church Youth Group. We thought it would be a great start to the school year. So while the boys were at school, Johnny and I could scramble around to get ready. I did a couple of chores—folding clothes into piles on the sofa and cutting tomatoes for canning—and then I would get ready to go out and run some errands. My mama was going to come with me because my doctor's appointment was at eleven up in Greenville, about an hour away, and then I planned to do some shopping in Anderson on the way back.

I was about to take a bath, but first I told Johnny that I needed some money to buy hot dogs, hamburgers, sodas, and everything else that we needed for the party. He retrieved his wallet from his blue-jean shorts and handed me a twenty-dollar bill.

"Just what are you thinking?" I said, putting the money down on a living room table. "That will probably feed five out of the thirty people that are coming!"

Johnny laughed. I knew there was no point in arguing with him. He was very tight with his money and it was like pulling teeth to get him to give me anything, so I sighed and proceeded to start my bath. As I walked to the bathroom, Johnny was walking out the door. But, several minutes later, I was sitting in the bath tub with shampoo in my hair and opened my eyes so see Johnny standing at the bathroom door. I jumped, startled, because I thought he had left. "What the heck are you doing? You scared me." I said.

"I thought I would come back and see you," he replied.

I thought that was a little crazy and out of character for Johnny and, besides, I was still mad at him about the money. I didn't respond. He left, and I finished my bath and then got ready to go. On my way out, I went back through the living room to pick up the twenty dollars he had left, and I finally understood. He had actually come back in to leave twenty more dollars. He had been teasing me—and it worked. But it left me with regrets about the last time I ever saw him alive. I wish I'd told him how much I loved him.

I left the house before ten, and Mama and I went to my eleven o'clock doctor appointment. Meanwhile, Johnny spent some time running errands and taking care of business around town. Since it wasn't unusual for him to be home in the middle of the day, he was likely to stop off at the S&S Party Shop. Everyone called it "the store" but, really, it was a community hang-out and bar that my parents owned. "S&S" stood for Stoney and Sue Parnell, my dad and mama. Stuart used to drop in several times a day and the place had a lot of regulars. In fact, Otis Compton, one of our neighbors, had been one. Up until August 6, Daddy used to see Otis around the S&S a good bit. After that, he never saw him there again.

That morning, Johnny dropped by the store at about ten o'clock to see my dad who had caught some fish earlier in the day. They chatted while they cleaned the fish, working at the water hose around on the side of the building. Even before noon, the day was a hot one. Johnny and Dad hung out at the S&S and talked with my father's friend, James Metz, from Iva. The bar wasn't busy at that time of day. Tonya Slaton was bartending and a few regulars, like one guy nicknamed Rubberhead, came in and out during the time Johnny was there. He left the bar by noon.

Mama and I stopped for lunch in Anderson, about half an hour north of home, and then ran more errands. Johnny went up to Anderson, too. Three minutes before one o'clock, he made a deposit at a Carolina First Bank branch there. He deposited three checks into our joint account, less three-hundred dollars, which he took in cash. After that, he stopped at a car wash, paying at 1:45 p.m., and then he headed home. While he probably planned to get some sleep before the party, I'm sure he also planned to do some work around the yard and the pool since he was extremely particular about everything being tidy and in order, especially for a party. No matter what else he was doing that day, I know he would have planned to be home before the bus dropped off the boys. As far as we know, Johnny was home around two o'clock.

Mama and I were still in Anderson. After lunch, we ran some errands to shop for the party and then we headed to a music store in Anderson so I could buy some church music.

Johnny pulled his truck off the driveway and parked under our Christmas cedar tree. From the front yard he couldn't see the vehicle behind the house. If only he had walked a few steps past the kitchen door, on the side of the house, to see what was going on in the backyard. If only. On a day like that, I wouldn't have been surprised if Johnny had headed straight for the pool to check the chemicals in the water. If only he had walked around to the other end of the house to the pool, he would have seen their vehicle and the open back door. If only.

Johnny didn't do any of those things. He went in the side door, as usual, and kicked off his shoes.

He would have seen them right away.

Johnny was not the kind of man who would shrink away from anyone, much less a bunch of scrawny guys who were ransacking his house. He would have moved to protect his home. He would have gone after them.

CHAPTER 6

A STRING OF BURGLARIES

IN FEBRUARY, MARCH, and April 1999, the area around our house had been hit hard by burglaries. South of our house, Charlie's Creek Road runs up from Lowndesville into the south side of Charlie's Creek Nursery, the large property just to the east of our place. Charlie's Creek Road runs along the lake, and several little dead-end roads and driveways brake off the old country road. Many of the houses back in there are lake homes and cabins, where people stay while they're enjoying the lake. Several of those houses had been ransacked for things that could be sold for cash—VCRs, TVs, video equipment, jewelry, and more unusual items like potato bins, irons, and household items. And there had been a string of burglaries along Highway 81, from Anderson County into Abbeville County, in Iva, Starr, and Lowndesville. Otis, his girlfriend Angel, and a guy named Blake had been arrested for those burglaries in April. According to police reports, the crimes stopped completely until Otis was released from jail on bail on July 27, just ten days before the murder.

It was during this time that I first heard that Otis Compton was using crack. Otis was in jail for four months awaiting bail. I thought after that much time away from doing crack that he wouldn't want to do it anymore, and this would be his opportunity to pay for what he had done and get his life back on track. But unfortunately, this was not the case. He and his buddies, Shane Rice and Robert Compton, are said to have parked along Mount Vernon Church Road in a secluded area about halfway between Iva and Lowndesville.

Working in 911, I had some training on dealing with people who use crack, but nothing compared to what I found out during my own research of the drug. I decided to research the drug mainly because I was seeing and hearing about some of my friends and other people getting addicted to this drug. I wanted to know what was so powerful that it could drastically change a person's morals. Crack addicts typically carry a little vile or folded scrap of paper filled with the small rocks that looked like cracked-off chips of soap. Emptying the rocks into their palms, the addicts would pack them into the glass tubes, their hands shaking as they lit the tube and burned the small rocks of cocaine. Finally, sucking in the first hit of smoke, their nerves would settle, calming their breathing.

I'm not exactly sure what took place on Mt. Vernon Church Road with Otis, Shane, and Robert, except for the fact that Otis told the police they were smoking crack. I guess, looking for the euphoria that crack addicts crave. It was a very hot day, but people who are on crack don't care or recognize how hot or cold it might be, because their body becomes immune to the oppression of the heat or cold.

Otis's daughter, Joy, was probably wrapping up her school day, about to get on the school bus with my boys, but Otis wouldn't have had room to think about his child if his brain was filled with crack. His marriage to Joy's mother, Tammy, hadn't lasted and he had been dating another woman, named Angel.

I met Angel years ago through a mutual friend. I always thought Angel was a pretty girl until I saw her several months before this day. I had already heard the gossip that she, too, was on crack. I learned that people who use crack acquire a particular look of sunken eyes, sores on their face, arms, and legs, and they appear to be nervous. When I saw Angel, she had that look to me. I knew she had some young children at home and I remember thinking how badly I felt for her children.

With Angel and Otis both using crack, I'm sure one of the main things on their mind was how to get money to buy more crack.

Though crack is considered the affordable form of cocaine, averaging ten to twenty dollars a rock in South Carolina, addicts need a steady stream of the drug to maintain the highs that their bodies crave. Crack cocaine alters the user's brain chemistry, quickly giving them a sense of euphoria, overinflated confidence, loss of appetite, insomnia, increased alertness and energy, and a craving for more cocaine. Most often, users smoke the drug because smoking efficiently delivers large quantities of the drug to the lungs, producing the immediate and intense euphoria. But a crack high lasts only five or ten minutes. After that, the brain's dopamine levels drop dramatically and the user feels depressed. Within a couple of hours, the high is completely gone and the user enters the "panic stage." He becomes desperate for another hit of the drug. But it gets worse. The dirty trick of crack cocaine addiction is that while the craving for that initial euphoria grows, the dopamine levels in the brain take a long time to replenish, and subsequent highs become less and less intense. As a result, users often binge for days and it quickly becomes a very expensive habit. All they care about is money. An addict will look for something—anything—to sell or pawn, even their own bodies. The craving is so intense that addicts think nothing of resorting to crime to fund their addiction.

South Carolina law enforcement officials report that crack cocaine is the drug most often linked with violent crime in the state. Many South Carolina agencies cite cocaine-related violent crime, trafficking, and abuse as the most serious criminal threat to the state.

Cocaine is extracted from the coca plant, which grows in South America. Cocaine consumed in South Carolina is produced in South America, and local street gangs and dealers convert the powdered cocaine into crack cocaine. Crack distributors prefer to convert powdered cocaine into crack near the area where they will sell it because federal sentences are harsher for possessing crack cocaine than for possessing powdered cocaine. While the media portrays crack as a problem in the inner cities, the poison has spread to rural areas, too.

Otis had long had a wild streak and the criminal record to go with it—DUIs, open container violations, and driving with a suspended license. As a seventeen-year-old eighth grader, Otis dropped out of school and worked a series of short-lived jobs at plants around the area before marrying Tammy and going to work doing occasional construction jobs for his father-in-law.

He lived about a mile from us in a trailer just down the road. Otis's small physique had dwindled to downright emaciated, probably due to his appetite for not much more than crack. He only weighed about 110 pounds. Shane Rice was also a little guy, scrawny at five-foot-seven and 130 pounds, while Robert Compton was a bit sturdier. With their sporadic work schedules, their usual dress was worn-out jeans and T-shirts. Personal hygiene and nutrition, I understand, are not a priority for crack addicts.

The police later said that Otis talked about getting hired back on at Crescent Mini Builders, a construction company he had worked at before his jail time. According to reports, Compton was not working then, either.

As the euphoria of the high wore off, the panic would have hit: *How can we get more crack?* Otis, Shane, and Robert left Mount Vernon Church Road and drove down the country road, according to court testimony. 22,000 They had a plan. Otis had seen some things inside our house.

A while back, Tyler had been selling candy for a fundraiser and he gave Otis's daughter, Joy, several pieces of it without collecting any money. I called the girl's mother and told her what Tyler had done, and asked if they could pay for the candy. Soon after that, Otis had brought Joy to our house to pay for the candy. Otis would have seen the gun cabinet that sat against the wall between our living room and master bedroom. Guns were valuable and easy to sell, and Otis would have known that Johnny's guns would score good money for plenty of rock.

The killers left Hilley Road and drove up the dirt track at the east end of our property. The dusty lane went up around the back of our land, up around behind the trailer, where they hid the truck from anyone passing by on the road. They parked on the lawn, up alongside the back porch, which was just a small wooden deck atop a few steps. Similar to the modus operandi in the lake house robberies, the killers used something like a crowbar to pry open the door to our utility room, and then they helped themselves to our life.

CHAPTER 7

DEATH

BY THE TIME Johnny walked into the house, the burglars had already gathered up a bunch of our family videos, taken my make-up bag from our bathroom, and retrieved a coffee can of money that we kept behind the headboard of our waterbed. They had already torn up our bedroom, throwing clothes out of the dresser and ransacking the whole room. They had already found the boys' piggy banks on my dresser and tried to get into the gun cabinet, messing with the panels of the doors.

As Johnny charged toward them, the burglars fought back. According to reports, the scrawniest one, Shane Rice, grabbed a bat and hit Johnny with it, but Johnny blocked the blow with his arm, taking the hit hard to his forearm. Johnny was so big that he hardly reacted. They fought some more, bumping into a window and breaking it from the inside. Rice ran through the utility room and out the back door. Johnny followed him. Before Johnny made it to the back door, he ran into someone else who waiting for him in the laundry room with a knife. The killer jabbed the knife underhanded into Johnny's neck, slicing his throat and chin, cutting all the way through to where his tongue was connected. The pathologist later reported that the force used would be like cutting into a thick steak. Blood poured from Johnny's neck.

As he fought, his blood dripped and pooled on the floor. Johnny grabbed for his assailant's arm and lunged forward at him, but the killer jabbed the knife into Johnny's chest. He jabbed again and again, trying to plunge the knife into Johnny's heart. Finally, he lodged it three inches into Johnny's chest. It stuck in the bones and muscle of Johnny's rib cage. According to the pathologist, the force of that stab was like cutting through a turkey drumstick with a steak knife.

With nothing but his own brute strength to defend against a bat and a knife, Johnny was still standing, still fighting back. As he was heading out the back door, still in pursuit, a shot rang out from the backyard, down on the ground. The bullet hit Johnny's right arm, blasting through and breaking the bones of his forearm, near his wrist. It may have been a defensive wound, an attempt to avoid a bullet after he saw a gun pointed at him. Johnny was still fighting. Our home was his pride, and he was not going to let it be violated. Another shot rang out, hitting Johnny in the abdomen. The bullet ripped into his rib cage, tore through his heart, and broke into his spine. The force knocked Johnny to the ground as blood sprayed the laundry room walls and dripped down the washing machine. Johnny was finally stopped by the bullet in his spine. He lay on his back, bleeding from two gunshots and three stab wounds, one through the heart. Though Johnny was no longer in pursuit, the shooter fired again. The bullet swept along his shirt, up into his jaw. Almost immediately, the shooter fired again, hitting Johnny in the neck. The bullet went up and tore into his brain, as blood splattered everywhere. Johnny could no longer fight.

Still, the nightmare continued.

The shooter climbed the steps up to the porch and stood in the laundry room doorway, over Johnny. He lay flat on his back, half inside, half outside, as the life drained out of him. His blood coursed out of his veins, painting the walls, and pooling around him. The shooter straddled Johnny—my husband, my sons' father. Standing directly over him, the killer pointed the gun at Johnny's left eye and fired again. Then, according to law enforcement, they rummaged around in his pockets, lifting him up to retrieve his wallet from his back pocket.

Finally, they left Johnny alone. Someone ran out across our field, while others got in the vehicle and drove it back down the track to Hilley Road and away.

As their daddy's heart beat its last, my boys were probably boarding the school bus with Otis Compton's daughter.

At 3:26, the 911 center at my office dispatched the emergency medical service and law enforcement to my house. My friend and colleague, Christi, listened to the helpless horror in Jeffrey's voice, but, still, she had to ask him to check on Johnny. For all she knew, he might have been fighting for his life, and Christi was trained to help callers save lives during emergencies.

But Jeffrey was in a state of pure terror. He pleaded with Christi, explaining that he could not go back into the laundry room. She said it was okay as she continued to talk to him while she sent out the dispatches. Now and then, Jeffrey whispered to Tyler, reminding him to be quiet in case the intruders were still around.

"Don't touch anything," she told my son. "Don't touch anything so we can find out what happened, okay, Jeffrey?"

My mama and I were in the music store in Anderson, selecting church music, when my pager went off. The page was from my office, Abbeville County 911 Dispatch, and it said, "Contact us as soon as possible. There is something wrong with your son." I was scared to death. What could have happened to Jeffrey or Tyler? And where was Johnny? Mama had a cell phone in the car, so we went outside and I called in. Keisha, who was on duty with Christi, answered my call. She told me that I needed to get home, that something was wrong at the house, and that the boys had come home and found Johnny unconscious and bleeding.

We got in my car, and I started to drive the twenty miles from Anderson. Since Johnny was so meticulous about keeping up the yard, I figured that he'd been doing something to get ready for the party and he'd gotten hurt. I thought maybe Johnny had been on that tractor and he rolled it, hit his head and been knocked unconscious. Since I'd worried about that in the past, it was the only thing I could think of. I had no idea. I didn't know how bad it was, but I knew it would take us every bit of thirty-five minutes to get home.

Since I was driving, I asked my mama to call the store to see if my dad was there and ask him to get to my house to check on the boys and Johnny. I could hear her part of the conversation as she asked the bartender to get Stoney, my dad, on the phone. She told him that I had gotten a call from work and they had said something was wrong with Johnny, that the kids had come home and found him with blood all over him, and the boys were having a fit. She told him that he needed to get over there and then she hung up. I drove the familiar highway toward Iva, and each mile seemed to take forever.

When he got the call, Dad had been talking with his friend, James Metz, who was still at the store. James agreed to go to the house with him. "But, Stoney," James cautioned as they walked toward the car. "We don't know what we're getting into here. You got a gun?"

"Got a rifle and a pistol in the store," said my father.

"Well, get that rifle," James said.

"I guess you're right," Dad nodded, running back into the store to get the gun. When he came back out, James had retrieved a .22 rifle from his truck and he got into the passenger side of Daddy's white Dodge sedan. Just as Dad got into the driver's seat of his car, Mot's husband, Stuart Baskin, pulled up. He agreed to come too, driving his own car. Stuart led the way.

The party store is less than two miles from our house, so it took Dad and the men just a couple of minutes to get there.

The boys heard sounds outside as the cars parked in front of the house. The men jumped out of the cars. Dad sprinted up the steps to the kitchen door but James and Stuart hesitated outside for a minute or two.

Hearing the kitchen door fly open as Dad bounded into the house, Tyler was shaking in terror.

Dad bolted into the kitchen. "Jeffrey?" he called. "Jeffrey? Tyler?"

Jeffrey hollered, "Back here, Papa! Back here!"

The boys were crouched in the corner near the couch. From his hiding place, my ten-year-old son pointed to the laundry room. "Back there, Papa," said Jeffrey. "Back there."

Thinking Johnny had fallen or had an accident around the house, My dad followed Jeffrey's gesture and walked across the living room. He peered around the wall into the laundry room, and stayed in the hallway as he knelt down to make sure that Johnny wasn't breathing. He saw the knife. Blood, all under Johnny and all over his face, had started drying. He could see a flesh wound on the right side of Johnny's neck.

"My Papa's here," Jeffrey said to Christi on the phone.

"Jeffrey," she said, "Don't let him touch anything, okay?"

"Okay," Jeffrey said, relaying the message.

Dad ran back to the kitchen door and looked out at James and Stuart. "Y'all come on in here!" he hollered. "And bring the gun. I don't know if somebody's still here or what, but this thing is worse than I thought."

James came in with the gun and Stuart went straight to the boys. Since Stuart and Mot had babysat Jeffrey and Tyler all their lives, they clung to them, wrapping their arms around them as they cried and trembled. Stuart sat on the couch, trying to comfort them.

My dad returned to the living room. "He's gone," he said.

"Papa!" Jeffrey said. "Papa, somebody wants to talk to you on the phone." Jeffrey tried a couple more times before Dad got on the phone with the dispatcher.

"Is Johnny breathing?" the dispatcher asked him.

"Nah," My dad answered. "He's done gone."

"Did you check his pulse?"

"No need to," said my dad. "His throat's cut wide open. Ain't no way that he's alive. He ain't breathing or anything."

On the way over, the Calhoun Falls emergency medical response team—

Stan Johnson, Darrell Manning, and Jan Johnson—realized they were going to my house. They had been there before, when my back had gone out and they had to transport me. Responding, the team prepared for the call, though it turned around on them a few times. At first, they thought they were going to assist someone with a head injury. Then they heard that the victim was unresponsive, then that it was cardiac arrest. With each update, they planned what they would face and how they would help. Finally, given the information they were getting, they knew that it must have been Johnny. All three of them knew Johnny, knew that he was my husband, and knew that we had two sons.

Still driving down from Anderson, I realized that we would be passing the hospital on our way home and I figured that we could meet the rescue squad there. I asked my mom to call the 911 Center and find out if the rescue squad had left with Johnny yet. I heard Mama's end of the conversation, but she didn't tell me right then that the emergency responders had requested the coroner.

After she hung up, she told me that the rescue squad had not left with Johnny, so I asked her to call Dad to check on him. Again, I only heard her side of the conversation. She asked Dad about Jeffrey and Tyler, but she didn't ask about Johnny because she already knew.

When she hung up, I asked her why she didn't ask about Johnny. "If you will pull the car over," she said, "I will tell you."

I knew in my heart that it was not good. I said, "Mama, please don't tell me that Johnny is dead."

"Sheila," she said, "pull the car over."

"What is it?" I asked. "What's going on?"

"Stop the car," she said.

I pulled the car to a stop and Mama got out and walked around to the back of the car.

"He's dead, isn't he?" I asked.

She nodded.

She took over driving. I immediately called our preacher, told him about Johnny, and asked him to go to the house.

Jeffrey heard the ambulance before Dad did and he took off outside. The vehicle was barreling down the road and slammed on their brakes as they missed the driveway. When my dad caught up with Jeffrey, he was outside, hollering for the rescue squad. "Come on in here," he yelled. "Come on in here!" He turned to my father. "Papa," he said, distraught. "They done missed the driveway!"

Dad thought that Jeffrey still believed his daddy was still living. Actually, Jeffrey realized that there was nothing they could do to help, but he felt infuriated, overwhelmed with anger. He later said that, if he had been old enough, he would have started a fight with anyone who got in his way.

The emergency medical service personnel—Stan, Darrell, and Jan— arrived at my home at 3:40, fourteen minutes after Jeffrey called 911. Stuart backed his car out of the driveway to make room for the ambulance, parking his car out on the road.

The paramedics, adrenaline pumping to save a life, rushed to the scene as fast as possible, first missing the driveway and then pulling in. Jan jumped out of the vehicle and asked Dad where to go. When he indicated the backyard, she ran around across the lawn, up the back steps, and up to the porch, still thinking that she could fix it, still thinking it was an injury accident. Then she saw all the blood, the body, the knife blade. It didn't take her but a few seconds to realize that Johnny had been murdered. Dale and Stan followed with the equipment and Jan saw them coming around the corner into the backyard. "Stop! Stop," she said. "Just stand there and look."

After shifting gears and dealing with their own emotions throughout the drive to the house, the medical crew was not prepared for what they saw. "It would have been bad for anyone," Jan Johnson remembered. "But to know the person made it ever harder." Seeing a husband and father brutally murdered and realizing that his small children had found him broke her heart. She went from a paramedic who could not change anything to a mother who was driven by instinct to protect the boys.

Jan could hear the boys crying. "Where are Sheila's boys?" she asked. Jeffrey answered, "We're in here."

Jan told him to get Tyler and both of them to come out the side door where she would be waiting for them.

Jan found Jeffrey "tore all to pieces," she said. Acting as if there was more he could do, Jeffrey gripped his fingers around that phone and wouldn't let go. "Honey," she said, "you've done all you were supposed to do. You can give me the phone."

Just minutes later, law enforcement arrived. The first officers to arrive at my house were John Gray and Sergeant Don Morris. It was Officer Gray's job to secure the scene. Since the medical crew couldn't do anything for Johnny and it was so hot outside, Jan asked Jeffrey and Tyler if they wanted to get into the ambulance which was cool with air conditioning.

Jeffrey looked suspiciously at the vehicle. "Is he in there?"

"No," she assured him.

Jan, Stan, and Darrell set up the boys in the back of the ambulance and gave them latex gloves to play with. They blew up the gloves with air and then drew silly faces on them. Tyler asked Jan to look in his school book bag and read the letter the teacher sent home. The letter said something like, "We are proud to have you in our class this year." It mentioned preparing for state testing in the first few weeks of school, and the last sentence said, "I hope you have a great weekend." *This is a weekend that these kids will never forget,* Jan thought.

Jeffrey turned to look at Jan and said, "I hope they get who did this to my daddy."

Jan's heart was breaking. "They will get who did this to your daddy," she said.

Jan, Stan, and Darrell couldn't comprehend that something so horrendous could happen in our small town, much less to someone they knew.

Officer Gray unrolled the crime scene tape and began securing the area.

He finished taping off the front yard as Detective David Alford and Chief Marion Johnson arrived somewhere around 3:40 p.m. Gray moved to the backyard to continue taping off the crime scene and Sheriff Charles Goodwin pulled in at approximately 3:45. Goodwin had been the county's elected sheriff for ten years, having worked his way up the ranks in the Abbeville Police force. He knew the area and he knew the people.

Goodwin walked around the back of the house. Johnny's body remained on the back porch, partially inside the back door to our double-wide mobile home. The window was knocked out. The back door was deformed, having been pried and twisted open. A knife blade lay across Johnny's chest.

Mama and I drove down Hilley Road just before four o'clock. As we neared my house, I noticed a good many parked cars lining our street. Up and down the road on both sides, people were out there, waiting and looking. Most of them were family and friends coming to be with us.

We finally arrived at the house. I got out of the car and paid no attention to the yellow crime-scene tape. I started to walk right through it, but a deputy stopped me.

"I need to get to my boys," I pleaded. "My boys are in there!"

Just then, I saw Jeffrey and Tyler walking toward me from the back of the rescue vehicle. The EMTs brought them out to the road, to me. Too young to realize the significance of what was going on at that moment, Tyler was excited to show me the blown-up plastic glove with faces on it while Jeffrey's little body seized with sobs. He cried hysterically. Both boys grabbed on to my body.

When the police allowed Stuart to leave he loaded the boys into his truck and drove off, but since the police had the road roped off, they wouldn't even let him and my boys go through to get back out to the highway. Stuart had to drive the long way around through the nursery. While they were driving, Tyler spotted three guys walking down the side of the road. "Maybe that's the guys that did it," he said.

"No, it ain't," Stuart assured him. "It ain't."

But all Tyler could think about was that those three guys were the murderers. He didn't know about the car tracks on the back lawn, or any of the other evidence. We didn't know anything at that time, and the boys were only picking up on things that they heard the bystanders talking about.

When they finally got to Stuart and Mot's house, the boys wanted to stay in the truck. They didn't want to go inside because they were too scared, afraid that the murderers might have been in the house. Instead, they stayed out in the yard, sitting and talking. In time, people stopped by, talking to Mot and Stuart about how Johnny was the kind of man who would take up for himself and protect what was his. The boys listened as people concluded that Johnny had the strength of two men. After hearing the conversations, Jeffrey decided that he was going to be just like his dad.

Marshall and Barbara were vacationing in Savannah, Georgia, so Johnny's cousin Tuck made the four-hour drive down to the coast to give them the devastating news. Tuck knocked on the hotel door, which Marshall opened. When Marshall saw Tuck, he knew it was bad news. Marshall spoke first. "Before you tell us anything," he said, "we need to pray." He and Barbara knelt together in prayer. When they were done, Tuck told them that they'd lost Johnny.

Long into the darkness, I stayed out in front of my house, sitting on the road outside the crime tape. At one point, Jan was standing beside me. "Jan," I said, "can you please go in there and help Johnny?"

She choked back tears. "There's nothing we can do, Sheila," she replied. "I am so sorry!"

CHAPTER 8
TWENTY MINUTES

CHIEF JOHNSON GATHERED all of the officers to discuss the homicide. Within twenty minutes, Otis Compton was the prime suspect in my husband's murder. Our back door had been pried at and kicked in, just like the doors in the nearby burglaries. Otis had been in jail for several months while the burglaries had almost completely stopped. During the week he'd been out, though, there had been two more burglaries in the area.

At 4:05 p.m., Goodwin called in an investigative team. Most small towns in South Carolina do not have their own full labs and investigative teams, so, according to protocol, Goodwin called to request assistance from the South Carolina Law Enforcement Division. SLED supports forty-six counties with crime scene processing and investigation.

Driving eighty-eight miles from Columbia, agent Michelle Dixon and two other agents arrived on the scene at 6:20 p.m. They maneuvered through the small crowd of people and media that had formed on our little country road. News of a murder was a big deal, and nobody could remember a murder in our area—ever.

Agent Dixon greeted the deputies, sheriff, and chief as she and her team got to work. She evaluated the security of the crime scene, did a walk through,

71

and then talked to Dad, James, and Stuart. They had to surrender their shoes so that investigators could compare them with any shoe imprints they might find. It was imperative that the crime scene and its evidence be protected and respected, to be sure that evidence was preserved. Everything needed to be photographed before being handled or moved. An expert in crime scene investigation, Dixon had completed two years of extensive hands-on and academic training with SLED after completing her criminal justice degree.

Gray brought the SLED team up to speed, and they began gathering evidence, avoiding disturbing the areas where the attackers had likely traveled. She entered the house from the kitchen door, working the crime scene backwards, as is protocol.

At one point, Agent Dixon asked me about my housekeeping standards. "It's important that I ask," she gently explained, "so I can know what things normally look like here."

I explained that I like to keep the house tidy, but that I had been doing laundry and there was some folded laundry on the couch as well as piles to be washed on the laundry room floor. Other than that, the house should have been neat, with everything in its place.

Dixon found the dining area, kitchen, and the boys' rooms tidy as usual, but when she entered the living area, she found it in disarray. The gun cabinet had obviously been messed with. And the master bedroom had been torn apart completely. There was a billy club on the bed and everything was overturned. Dixon snapped pictures of it all.

Then she moved toward the back door and Johnny's body. Her eyes scanned from floor to ceiling, seeing blood splattered everywhere. A video camera and a bunch of tapes that had been taken from the living room were dropped in the utility room. A serrated knife blade, missing its handle, rested on Johnny's chest. She photographed it from a general range and close up. Along with all of the other items of evidence, the knife blade would be collected, labeled with the lab number, an item number, her initials, and the date, and taken back to the lab in Columbia for processing. There, the blade would be treated with a protein dye stain called amido black to enhance the blood, turning it a darker shade to show any ridge detail in finger prints that may have been left.

Johnny was wearing shorts with a white Polo shirt and no shoes. His shoes were by the door, which was his routine. His clothes were soaked with blood. She looked at the injuries, though it was difficult to see all of them because Johnny was a large man and there was so much blood. She noted the pool of blood that had formed around his head. It was deep. Dixon used a tool to rake through the blood so she could see if any evidence was submerged in the blood. She found a bullet, completely hidden in the pool of blood near Johnny's head. She marked it for the lab. Since the utility room was small and his body straddled both inside and out, she stepped outside and studied Johnny from another perspective. She took more photos of the blood splatter, the back door, the bedroom, the broken window, and everything in the room.

With the crime scene recorded in photographs, and the evidence bagged and labeled, Johnny's body was put into a body bag and loaded onto a gurney. Agent Dixon swiped each of his palms, front and back, to test for gunshot residue, using a prepackaged gunshot residue kit with sticky stubs and swabs labeled for each part of the hand—left back palm, left palm, right back palm, right palm, and so on. It would be important later, so that they could identify whether any lead was left on Johnny's hands. After completing the GSR kit, Dixon fingerprinted Johnny. Finally, at about midnight, his body was removed to the coroner's office.

In the backyard, the investigators had identified a spot that might have indicated vehicle tracks, so they photographed the area and tried to make castings of it. Though it was obviously dug out from a vehicle driving through the yard and pushing down the grass, the team was unable to get a casting impression. To be thorough, they made castings of the EMS vehicle's tires so that they could compare that to the prints.

While the investigators continued gathering evidence into the night, I left what was once our perfect home and headed to my parents house. We never slept at that house again.

Richard Stone lived a couple of miles from us, where our road eventually came out to Highway 81. On Saturday morning, August 7, he was outside of his house, picking up trash along the highway. He routinely picked up trash for about a quarter of a mile down the road from his house, both ways.

While he was cleaning up the shoulder of the road, Stone saw a wallet lying on the ground with several pieces of paper around it. He picked up the wallet. Opening it, he reached in with his thumb and eased the card up to see the picture and name—Johnny Hanna. Stone didn't know Johnny personally, but by Saturday, everyone in town knew the significance of the name. News of the murder shocked Iva and Lowndesville. Stone laid down the wallet right where he'd found it. He went straight home and called the Sheriff's Department.

Sheriff Goodwin called Detective Alford and the two men drove out to Richard Stone's house in the remote area outside of Lowndesville. Alford put on latex gloves, bent down, and thumbed open the wallet. He looked at the identification. It was Johnny's, all right. It had no cash in it. Alford photographed the location of the wallet and bagged it as evidence.

At the coroner's office, the autopsy was started. At our house, Chief Johnson walked through the crime scene again.

CHAPTER 9

A FAMILY OF THREE

SOME PEOPLE SAY that in every event or circumstance, there is a dessert to be found. Of course, it seemed impossible to find the dessert in Johnny's death but, as we dealt with the realities of it, I realized that if it hadn't been the first day of school, my boys would have been with Johnny. I kept thinking that I could have lost my whole family that day, not just my husband. So I realized that this was the dessert.

As I sat outside my house with Mama in the darkness that night, my sister Sherri came down and found us sitting there outside the police tape, waiting. Nine months pregnant, Sherri had sent her husband, Doug, to get some take-out burgers, which they took up to Stuart and Mot's for Jeffrey and Tyler. By about nine that night, Sherri and Doug had taken my boys home with them.

Jeffrey had a special relationship with my brother, Jamie, and wanted to spend the night at his house, so Jamie and his wife Kristie picked up Jeffrey and took him home with them. They'd had the television on and Jeffrey saw a teaser come on the news. It was quick, but said that two sons had found their dad dead. Intrigued by that, Jeffrey didn't feel upset by it so much as a little strange—weird—that here we were, going through the biggest crisis of our lives, and the television station was using it to get attention for the news. As for me, I felt like it was a good thing because I hoped that the publicity would help the investigation, making people aware and mindful about who might have done it.

Tyler spent that night with Sherri and Doug and their kids, who were close in age to my boys. Tyler was afraid to sleep in his cousin's bedroom and asked if they could sleep in the living room, outside Sherri and Doug's room, instead. Sherri was fine with it. She put a cot on the floor and Tyler and his cousins fell asleep, and then Sherri and Doug also went to bed and tried to sleep.

At some point during the night, or maybe in the early morning hours, Sherri was restless. She dreamed that a bright light was shining on the living room ceiling, shining into her bedroom. It was the light of angels—so bright that it hurt her eyes—so she kept trying to roll over and change positions so that the glaring light wouldn't shine in her eyes. Sherri just couldn't get her eyes closed enough to fall asleep. She was dreaming, but it felt real, as if angels were visiting her home. She was so disturbed by the light, that she even got up out of bed and went to the living room to look around and see what it was, but everything was normal and everyone was asleep, so she went back to bed and tried again to go back to sleep. But, as soon as she fell asleep, the bright light was there again, pouring from the living room into her bedroom. She got up again, two or three times, and finally sank back into bed and fell asleep, and it finally seemed like the dream of angels in her living room was gone and done. "I don't know what it was," she later said. "I guess it was a dream."

The next morning, Tyler came up to Sherri. "Aunt Sherri," he said, "do you believe in angels?"

"Yeah," Sherri said.

"Well," little Tyler said. "I think my daddy and angels were here last night with me."

Tyler told her that he was able to sleep because he knew that his daddy was okay.

When I came to get Tyler, Sherri told me about the dream. She felt that it was important for me to know because it would help me believe that Johnny was okay, that he was with the angels. We didn't tell very many people because we figured they would think we were crazy..

I gathered my children and took them to my parents' house. We were wrecked, so terrified that it was even hard to grieve over Johnny. We had no idea why he was murdered and, for all I knew, we might have still been targets. I couldn't imagine any possible reason why anyone would go after Johnny, so I didn't see why the killer would stop there. I feared that they would come back to finish the job. To make it even worse, I heard a rumor that the killers may have thought that Jeffrey and Tyler had seen them when they got home from school. That terrified me. What if the people who killed Johnny heard that my sons had been on the scene? What if they believed that Jeffrey and Tyler had witnessed the crime or seen the killers? They would come after Jeffrey and Tyler! My children would be targets, too. To ease my mind, the Sheriff's Department put a police car in front of my parents' house, but it did little to quell our panic.

Jeffrey was especially frozen with fear. He had a hard time going into my family's homes, and was scared to enter any room alone. Any house seemed as if it could have harbored a shocking horror or a murderer, and every doorway could have revealed a bloodbath. Jeffrey couldn't go indoors by himself, couldn't walk from one room to another alone, not even into the bathroom. I knew the fear that Jeffrey and Tyler were feeling because I was scared to go into other rooms by myself as well.

As I did the work of planning the funeral services, I struggled with my feelings. Nothing made sense to me. Johnny was a good person and his death made me question why bad things happen to good people. Since Johnny and I had just turned our lives around and started to lead the right life—living for Him—it made no sense to me that God would take Johnny from me. I felt so full of anger, overwhelmed by it, and I was angry at God.

The day brought a morbid parade of family, friends, and strangers, who brought us food and condolences. It seemed as if we saw everyone who knew us, as well as folks whom we'd met only once in our lives. Even the boys' bus driver came to see us. She felt so bad, blaming herself for letting the boys off that day, but how could she have known anything of the horror inside our normal-looking house? She had no way of knowing that, on that day, nothing was normal. The next year, though, as a result of my sons' trauma, the school district passed a rule that bus drivers were not to let off a child unless there was a parent or guardian at the bus stop to meet them, or at least in physical sight of the driver.

That afternoon I wanted to be by myself, so I went outside and sat on the porch. A wonderful Christian lady, whom I respect very much, came outside to see me. "Sheila," she said, "you know, this was God's plan. Something good will come from this."

I could not get past the first part of her statement. I kept thinking about such a God. God knew this was going to happen, yet He allowed it to happen? I kept thinking, *What kind of God would do that?* I directed even more anger toward God. I wanted Him to tell me why He let it happen. Why did He leave my boys without their daddy? Why did He leave me without my husband? Why, if He loved us so much, did He allow something so awful to happen to us? This was the start of a big struggle in my Christian faith. It took me several years to understand what this woman was telling me that day, and my comprehension of those words then and now is totally different. Throughout my journey Johnny's father, Marshall, helped me find comfort in my faith. Though he had already suffered great family tragedy, Marshall's faith had survived. He told me that I couldn't blame God for Johnny's death. He told me that God was right here with us, helping us cope. He talked to me many times, assuring me that God was at work in my life. "Sheila, don't give up on God," he said, "because He will never give up on you." Marshall kept telling me things, not giving up on me. I would listen, but it was a struggle for me to really hear and understand what he was telling me.

Marshall and Barbara had raised three children, two sons and a daughter, but Johnny was the second son they lost. Blake was the first. He killed himself in 1979 and the family had long suffered with unresolved pain. It was hard for me to understand how they dealt with it.

Whenever we visited Johnny's parents, I noticed that they never had any pictures of Blake displayed on the walls of their home and that they never talked about him. His name was hardly ever brought up. I thought that was kind of odd.

One day, before we lost Johnny, he said, "Sheila, I really want to know what happened to Blake."

"What do you mean, what happened to him?"

"Blake left a note," Johnny explained. "And I want to know what it said."

"You should, ask your mama and dad."

"No," he said. "They don't have it. The Sheriff's Office has it."

Since I was a 911 telecommunicator for the county, he asked me to go and see if they would give me a copy of the note.

"Johnny," I said, "I don't think they'll give it to me because I was not part of the family then, but they'll give it to you."

I never found out if he really wanted to know about the note. I have wondered if he thought making an attempt to find out would help him heal from the loss. He did not try to retrieve the note, and did not mention it to me again.

The next Thanksgiving, we had dinner at Barbara and Marshall's and I noticed the family pictures. Barbara had put some pictures of Lynn, Johnny, and their families out on the wall and on a couple of side tables, but no pictures of Blake were out.

When I got the opportunity with Barbara, I made a suggestion about the pictures. "Barbara," I said. "You know what would be really neat on your wall? A picture of Johnny, Blake, and Lynn on this wall, and then on this wall you could split up your family, your grandkids, and things like that."

She didn't respond but, when we went back to their house a few weeks later, I noticed that she had Blake's picture on the wall.

After we left, I mentioned it to Johnny. "Did you notice that your mama had Blake's picture up on the wall?" I asked.

"Yeah," he said. "That's a first."

"How could you never talk about Blake?"

"It makes them so sad," he said. "I guess that's the reason why we never talk about him."

Still, Marshall was a man of deep faith, and he helped me as I struggled to understand God's hand in our tragedy. While I wasn't sure what I believed, I had to remember that Johnny and I had agreed that we were going to raise our boys in the church. It was like I was fighting. I wanted to feel and do what Johnny wanted, but at the same time I didn't want anything to do with it. And here I was, trying to plan Johnny's funeral.

For days I wasn't allowed back in my house, so we were stuck without anything, not even toothbrushes. The only clothes we had were the clothes we'd been wearing that day. Sherri loaned me some clothes to wear and I had to borrow clothes for the boys and, then, I had to go buy them clothes to wear to Johnny's funeral.

We slept together in the comfy chairs in my parents' living room, and Tyler often woke up with nightmares, screaming and hollering. That happened a lot. We were all frightened and on edge. A day after Johnny was killed, somebody had stolen a vehicle out of a yard near Sherri's house and crashed the car into a building. There was a lot of commotion with law enforcement vehicles all around and I was terrified, thinking it had to be the same people who had killed Johnny. These kinds of crimes—murders and car thefts—didn't happen around Lowndesville. I was convinced that whoever had stolen the car was the same person who had killed Johnny, and I was terrified. Even when there were no other crimes happening in the area I was always terrified, and so were the boys.

Next to the fear, I struggled a lot with the fact that the last time I had seen

Johnny alive, I had been annoyed with him about leaving me only twenty dollars for the party food. I regretted that so much, and suffered a great deal because I wondered—and would always wonder—whether Johnny knew how much I loved him. I knew that he knew, but I couldn't let go of an inkling of doubt in part of my heart. He was taken from me so suddenly and I didn't have the opportunity to let him know—really let him know—how much I totally loved him. That started haunting me from the first day.

After we lost Johnny, I told the boys that we had to always say that we love each other whenever we say goodbye. I said that, if we feel that way, we have to make sure the other person knows it. Jeffrey and Tyler and I have done that ever since. Whether we talk on the phone or we leave one another's company, we always part by saying, "I love you." It means a lot to me.

CHAPTER 10

CLOUDY DAYS

IN PREPARING FOR the funeral services, I wanted to get Johnny's wedding ring so that he could be buried with it on his finger. I asked the investigator if he could retrieve Johnny's wedding band from my jewelry box, on my dresser. He told me that they hadn't seen a jewelry box in my bedroom. The burglars had stolen it, with Johnny's wedding ring and mine, too.

At the time, I didn't have the money to go and buy Johnny a cheap ring, but I didn't want him to be buried without a wedding band. As it happened, Sherri had just bought her husband, Doug, a new wedding band for his birthday and they still had his old one. "Sheila," she said, "I really would be honored for you to put that one on Johnny. You want a wedding band. That will be my part." I was so grateful.

The Calhoun Falls Funeral Home Director called that Sunday morning and told me that they were ready for me to come and view Johnny's body, to make sure everything was the way that I wanted it. This would be the first time that I would see Johnny since the episode in the bathroom two days earlier. The boys did not want to go to the funeral home for this and I didn't make them. I walked into the room with Sherri, my Aunt Wanda, and my mom walking beside me. I saw Johnny's casket at the far end of the room, and a few of Johnny's cousins were already there.

I'm not sure what was going through my mind but I know that I was not prepared to see Johnny in a casket. As I approached him, my legs began to get weak. As soon as I got close enough to see his face and body, my emotions overwhelmed me. I froze. I tried to remain strong, but, when I saw him, the reality hit me. I didn't know that one person could feel so many emotions all in an instant. I wanted to run up to Johnny and have him tell me that it was all a joke, that he was fine. The next minute, I wanted to hit him for leaving me and the boys. Then I wanted to hug him and tell him I loved him, and that I was so proud of him for the stand he took to protect our home. All these thoughts and feelings ran through my head, swirling around.

"Sheila?" my aunt said. "Are you okay?"

No, I thought. *I am not okay. I don't understand why I'm here or why Johnny is here. If someone can explain how we got to this point and the reason behind it, then I might be okay.* I didn't say what I was thinking. I dug deep in my heart and spoke. "Yes," I said, without hesitation. "I'm fine." But I had no idea what those four words even meant.

I approached the casket and stood next to Marshall, Barbara, and Lynn. I couldn't think of anything to say, and the only thing that came to mind was practical. "I think we need to have them put a tie on Johnny," I blurted. I felt that I needed to be strong for them and for my boys. I didn't want to show weakness because I knew that they all needed me to be strong, and I knew that Johnny would have expected it—at least, that is what I thought.

As I turned to walk away, Sherri handed me the wedding band. I asked the funeral home director if he would put it on Johnny's hand and add a tie to his shirt. We left.

That night, we went back for the friends and family viewing before anybody else got there, so that we could be with the body first. Right off, I noticed that the band was on Johnny's ring finger...on his right hand!

"Sherri," I whispered, "they have the wedding band on the wrong hand!"

I had never touched a dead person before and, even though it was Johnny,

I could not pick up that ring. Sherri said she wouldn't mind switching it to Johnny's left hand, and she did. She removed the ring and put it on his other hand, so Johnny was buried with a wedding band. It wasn't the one I gave him, but he was buried with a wedding band all the same.

Since Jeffrey and Tyler did not want to come to the funeral home, they stayed with our best friends, Tommy and Gayle Brown. Our family viewing was from six to eight o'clock that evening, but the weather was still so hot. The funeral home was crowded with people in the building and the air conditioner couldn't pull for so many, so it was uncomfortable inside and out. At one point, Mama and I went outside so I could smoke a cigarette and I saw the line of people, streaming out the building. I walked out to my car to get my cigarettes and I could see the long line of people leading down the sidewalk.

"Mama," I said. "Look at all the people that are here."

At that moment, I began to understand the impact of Johnny's death on our town. Just after Johnny's murder I had known that people in Lowndesville were deeply affected, but to see all the people from Iva and Lowndesville and Calhoun Falls, I was amazed. If I had stayed inside the whole time, seeing everyone as they came through the line, it wouldn't have hit me as much as it did when I saw that line of people standing out in that heat. They had to have known that they were going to be in that line for an hour or more, and still they stood there, waiting. That's when I knew how many lives Johnny had impacted. That's when I realized that the impressions he made on people will last their lifetimes.

Sometimes, I see some of the guys who were friends with Johnny and still, more than ten years after his death. They'll get to talking about him and I'll see them tear up. "You know," they might say, choking up, "you couldn't ask for a better friend than Johnny."

It was almost midnight before we left the funeral home.

As a mother, I wanted my sons to see Johnny all cleaned up so that, maybe, their final and lasting image of him wouldn't be the horror that they saw in our laundry room. I knew that the sterile and doughy impression of their father, lying in the satin billows of his casket, was contrived, sculpted, and unreal, but at least there was no bloodbath, no knife, no wounds. But there were.

On the day of the funeral, I called the funeral home director and asked if I could bring the boys to the church after they placed Johnny's body there. I explained to him that they had not attended the viewing the night before and that it was very important to me that they see their father cleaned up. I didn't know how the boys would react when they saw Johnny, so I also asked the funeral director if he would ask the guests to wait outside for a few minutes while we allowed the boys some time with their dad. He obliged, and within the hour we went to the church so that the boys could see their dad for the first time since that Friday afternoon.

For Jeffrey the viewing made it seem as if Johnny was sleeping, though the body didn't look like Johnny normally did, of course. To Jeffrey, he looked white, pasty. It wasn't so hard, Jeffrey said, but it wasn't good, either.

For Tyler, it was plain bad. At the family viewing, only a very few close family members were present. Tyler, Jeffrey, and I walked up to the casket, and as soon as we reached Johnny's body, Tyler stepped around to the far side of the coffin. He looked down at his father's neck and saw the marks, like holes, down behind and below Johnny's ear.

"Ugh," Tyler sniffed, disgusted. "It's still there."

I was shocked. Tyler still remembers wondering what it was. He says he asked me several times about those things on Johnny's neck and recalls that I wouldn't ever tell him what it was.

It was a bullet hole.

I knew little about funeral homes and how they prepare a body, but I had assumed that all of Johnny's wounds would have been hidden. I felt sick that the wound was still there, and that Tyler had seen it.

I was also a little confused. I knew that Jeffrey had seen the body but he did not see Tyler look into the laundry room, and we thought—assumed—

that Tyler had been spared. When he said, "It's still there," I had to wonder: had my six-year-old seen the horror?

Planning the service—with the right music—was very important to me. It seemed bigger than me, like a responsibility. I picked out appropriate songs for the funeral; "Go Rest High on that Mountain" by Vince Gill and then "Cloudy Days" and "My Hope Appeared" by Jeff Collier. Jeff is a church friend who is also a singer/songwriter, but more like a singer/preacher. He has touched me deeply.

When I picked "Cloudy Days," in my mind I was thinking that it would send a message to everybody in the community who needed to hear from Johnny. People were devastated and scared and I knew that Johnny wouldn't want people to live like that. He would want them to remember that this was just one cloudy day, and that we shouldn't let it dictate our outlook. I felt that the community needed to know that, if Johnny could have said anything to them, he would have said that we don't give in to a cloudy day but we deal with it and then move on. The spiritual part of this was that Johnny had moved on. Though he'd experienced his cloudy day, he was fine now.

"Cloudy Days"

I woke up this morning, looked out my window, to find another cloudy day
Not a ray of sunshine
All my troubles seemed to stare me face to face
But there's something about this cloudy day
Cloudy days only serve to remind
That long ago the Savior hung on the cross that was mine
So when dark clouds hide your view
Remember Jesus has been there too
Cloudy days can never stop His sunshine
Long ago on a hill in a far away land
Stood an old bloody cross where the sin debt was gladly paid

And when the Father turned His face
Dark clouds rolled in that day
You see Jesus knows all about cloudy days...

I chose the other Jeff Collier song, "My Hope Appeared", because it fit Johnny's life so literally, from the time before he had a relationship with God until the day he died. Again, this was a message that I wanted to convey to others because it said that, regardless of what you have done in your life, God is your hope. I knew that, on the day he died, Johnny saw that hope appear and he went to heaven.

"My Hope Appeared"

Going down with no way up
I had to drink my bitter cup
Reaping the harvest that I had sown
When I knew I'd reached the end
There hung Jesus bearing my sin on an old rugged cross
Yes my hope appeared on an old rugged tree
In glimmering light to my surprise He came to rescue me
On an old rugged tree
Looking back I can see those tender hands holding me
They were caring when no one really cared
And all the while leading me to the grace of Calvary
That's where hope appeared for me

I wanted the community to take the sermon of this song to heart. I realized, too, that I picked this song because I needed to hear it; its message was as much for me as for anyone else. The words of this song served to remind me that no matter how bad things were, God was my hope. I think I knew what I needed, and sensed and assumed that the community needed the same thing.

It was like I was trying to preach to the choir, reminding myself that Johnny was talking to me, saying for me to do this. It was as if I was trying to serve others and, in doing so, I was also serving myself.

After the funeral, people told me that they thought it was a great service, not just the traditional stuff, but that it had honored Johnny. They're right, and I liked that because I felt like I was honoring him, largely with the words of the Jeff Collier songs. Through the music I was trying to let people know that Johnny was a good person and that, if he was standing here, he would say, "Don't let this stop you. Don't let life in Lowndesville stop because of what happened to me."

Johnny was buried in Smyrna Cemetery in Lowndesville. Since we were a young couple, we had not prepared for death. Johnny actually had a life insurance policy but it was quite small and only came about because he and my dad had been drinking when the life insurance salesman was around, pushing policies. "You need to get this life insurance," Dad kept telling Johnny. Then, he'd turn to the salesman and add, "Tell him how cheap it is." Johnny ended up taking out a small policy, which he had when he died, but it wasn't even enough to cover all of the costs of his funeral and burial. I didn't know what to do about getting him a burial plot.

When I was a teenager my dad had acquired five plots at the Smyrna Cemetery, which was public. People don't purchase plots there, but instead come and rope off what they want. That's all it takes; it's theirs. My dad had come and roped off a big enough plot for the five of us—Mama, Dad, my brother, my sister, and me. But when Johnny died, I couldn't afford to have him buried at the cemetery where his brother is buried, and I didn't know what to do or where to bury him. Then Mama and Dad gave me half of their plot at Smyrna, so Johnny was the first person to be buried in my family's plot.

In the days and weeks after the funeral, though, I was too scared to take the boys to the cemetery. I was afraid for us to be by ourselves anywhere because, for all I knew, somebody—the murderer—could be there. A few times my dad came with me to bring the boys to visit Johnny's grave, and Mama went with me sometimes, too. I just wanted to come down for a visit, but I was too afraid to go there alone. When we did go, we couldn't sit and have a quiet, peaceful moment because we were constantly looking around to see if anyone was around or if anyone was coming.

About a week after Johnny died, I got a call from the director of the recreational league where Jeffrey and Tyler played baseball. He asked me if the boys and I would be okay if they did a moment of silence to honor Johnny, who had been one of the coaches, before the last game of the season. I told him it would be nice.

When we got to the field, large banners were hanging on the big fences across the outfield. They said, Coach Johnny, we will always remember you, We are Praying for the Hanna Family, and things like that. Then, the two teams had a moment of silence to remember Johnny. Since nobody knew who had killed him, and there was a rumor going around that Jeffrey and Tyler had seen the killer, officers from the Calhoun Falls police stayed at the field the whole time, keeping an eye out.

After that, Tyler quit playing baseball. He didn't want to play sports anymore because Johnny had always been his coach.

We tried to carry on with life as best we could. Sherri and Doug invited us to a big barbecue that Doug's dad had on his property every year, on the first Saturday of August. Johnny and I had gone to it a few times, and the boys had, too. Doug's dad had started having the annual party, with a live band and dancing, about forty years earlier, inviting his friends, neighbors, and people he worked with. Over the years the party grew, as his kids grew up and invited their friends and families, and then the grandchildren grew up and married and started inviting their friends and families. Usually, two or three hundred people attended the barbeque.

But after Johnny died, the boys could not enjoy it. They felt like everybody was staring at them. Jeffrey kept saying, "What if the person that killed my daddy is here? They might get me." The boys were even too scared to go in the bouncy house that was there. I was stressed out, too. People would come up to me and give me their condolences, but other people didn't talk to me at all because they didn't know what to say. I looked at everyone, wondering if they knew anything. It was a hard day and really too much for us. We left early and headed back to my parents' house.

All three of us were so scared, but Tyler was curious, too. He asked a lot of questions. Jeffrey wouldn't even talk. He could not be alone at all, and when light shone into a room in a certain way, it scared him. He slept on the couch next to my dad.

Johnny's death was making headlines, at least locally. By August 11 our newspaper, *The Press & Banner,* reported that the sheriff believed that Johnny's death "occurred in connection with a burglary." As we came to believe these reports—and learn more about them—it helped calm our rational and reasonable fears about being targets. But at the same time, my children suffered a great deal from another kind of fear.

Jeffrey was constantly scared. Everywhere he went, he looked over his shoulder. As we settled in at my parents' house we still slept on chairs in the living room. Jeffrey was afraid to sleep in a bedroom. He was also still afraid to go into any room or house alone. If he was around people or in a public place he was fine, but he was terrified when he was by himself or walking into a private residence.

At the same time, he seemed to assume an innate sense of stoicism and responsibility. He was now the man of the house. Though Jeffrey was only ten years old, Johnny had taught him that this was his role. "I felt like I had to be the one to take care of us," Jeffrey said. "Obviously Daddy couldn't do it and somebody's got to do it, and so it had to be me."

Several days after Johnny was killed, one of the SLED investigators took me to the house so that I could provide more information about the condition of the house and list stolen property before they turned the house back over to me. This was the first time that I saw the condition of our ransacked bedroom, although it also seemed like the police had crudely dumped things back into the closet and into the dresser drawers, maybe in an effort to tidy up. I started digging through our belongings, which were spilling out from the dresser. Among them, I saw a man's brown leather glove. I picked it up between my thumb and forefinger as if it were a dirty rag. For an instant, I dangled it above the drawer. "This is not ours," I blurted as I dropped it and jumped back, realizing in that moment where it had come from.

With the investigators, we pieced together a list of items that were missing from my home. That list included:

- A can of cash
- Johnny's wallet and about $300 in cash
- Jeffrey and Tyler's piggy banks
- My jewelry box
- All of my jewelry, including my one-third carat diamond cluster engagement ring with a gold wedding band
- Johnny's jewelry, including his father's thirty-year service watch from Rocky River Mill, and a four-diamond square man's ring;
- Johnny's gold wedding band
- My makeup case and makeup
- Most of our home video tapes as well as movies and children's videos

We did not see the autopsy results for quite some time but the information was important to the investigation and revealed a great deal about what happened. For me, it showed that Johnny fought—and fought hard. It also showed me that the killer had wanted him dead.

Johnny was stabbed several times. Though my impression was that those wounds were not fatal, the nature of the wounds suggested that Johnny was moving when he was stabbed, or the killer was turning the knife during the attack. Johnny's stab wounds included several superficial cuts on his chest, near his heart, and investigators thought that these quick repeated stabs indicated that the killer was trying to attack Johnny's heart. But few of these wounds were deep, and it looked like Johnny had overpowered the attacker.

He was, however, no match for the gun. Remarkably, he held up and fought for his life while a bullet tore up the bones of his forearm. That bullet, or another, ripped through the flesh of his abdomen, flew through his diaphragm, ripped through both sides of his heart, and then sliced upward through the central part of the inside of his chest—through his main arteries and bronchi—until it penetrated and lodged into his spine. Large and strong, Johnny endured the pain and fought for his life. Bullet after bullet after bullet tore through his body, stopping him and ultimately killing him.

Finally, Johnny might have tried to turn away as another bullet crashed through his jaw and tore up through his head, behind his face, until it lodged inside his forehead. Another one, also intended to kill, ripped through his neck and into the left side of his brain, splintering his skull. The final shot into my prone, dying, and helpless husband, entered near his eye, destroying his brain.

By my understanding of the report, Johnny was alive when he was shot in the heart, and he was alive when the bullets blasted through his head. Because he was so big and so strong it took a lot to kill him, but he did finally lose the fight. Against a gun, he never really had a chance.

On the day of the murder, I had been doing laundry. I had folded some clothes into piles on the couch and sorted the dirty laundry into piles on the laundry room floor. It had been under the blood. I didn't think about it but, before the officials allowed us back into our house, the State had cleaned up most of the blood in the utility room—though some blood remained up on the ceiling—and they had laundered all of those clothes. When we moved our stuff out, I took the piles of clothes. It didn't hit me that some of those clothes had been soaked with Johnny's blood, with his life, with his death. Had I realized it, I would have burned them. But, by the time it hit me, we had been wearing the clothes for about a month, and I had no idea which clothes had been on the floor and which ones had already been folded. I couldn't do anything about it, other than feel sick.

Once the police allowed us back into our house, we moved our beds and some personal belongings over to my parents' house. It took a few trips. One day, I had the boys with me in Johnny's truck and we were headed over to the house to get some more stuff out of our house. Jeffrey rode next to me while Tyler was asleep on the back seat. I called my dad and asked him to meet me there, because I was afraid to go in by myself. I was driving out Hilley Road and nearing the house when a car came toward us, speeding. As soon as it passed our truck, the car slammed on its brakes, pulled over, and started to make a three-point U-turn.

I was scared to death. I thought it could be Johnny's murderer, coming after us. I drove right past our driveway. At the far end of our property, I slammed on the brakes and yanked the wheel to turn the front of the truck into the dirt track, to turn the truck where the school bus turned around. I hit a ditch and bounced back out of it without even slowing down. Tyler, still asleep, fell onto the floor. Both boys popped up to watch the commotion and I kept pushing them back down. *They're gonna start shooting,* I thought. *Get the boys down onto the floor!*

Leaving a trail of dust, I passed our house again and sped back toward the highway. I met the car again. I was flying when I reached the end of the road, near Stuart and Mot's house. Just then, I saw my dad turning into Hilley Road from the highway. I stopped sharp.

"Turn around," I said. "Get out of here!"

I took off and raced to the party store. Mama was there and I had her call 911. After a few minutes, Dad still had not come back. I was terrified. It probably wasn't long, but it seemed like an hour. "They're gonna do something to Dad," I kept telling Mama. "They're gonna do something to him!"

Finally, he showed up at the party store. He said that he had seen the car and was waiting to see what the driver was doing.

The police showed up and I described the car. One officer recognized the description of the car as belonging to a man that had been at the store in Lowndesville earlier. The officers went to the man's house and asked him if he had been driving the car.

"No," the guy said.

The police felt the hood of the car, which was still warm. "I'm gonna ask you again," the officer said. "Have you been driving that car?"

"No," he repeated.

"I know that you were because I was just at the store in Lowndesville and you pulled in, in that car," said the officer.

"Yeah," the man finally admitted. "I've been driving it."

"Were you on Hilley Road?"

"Yeah, I was," he said.

The police officers determined that the guy didn't have a driver's license and had been out joy riding. He wasn't after me or my boys or anything like that. But how could I know? It was scary. Everything was scary. The officer and the Sheriff tried extremely hard to make me understand that this man was not after us, but at the time, I couldn't believe that. Although I trusted the Sheriff and everyone working on the case, I couldn't get past my fear for myself and my boys. There was nothing they could have said that would have convinced me that this incident had nothing to do with Johnny.

One night, as Tyler and I were lying in bed, he asked me why God took Daddy from us. I wanted to explode. I had been asking this very question to myself. I felt as if I was fighting to keep my faith, and trying to understand what happened. Although at times I blamed God, I did not want my boys to feel that same anger. Deep down I knew that God was not responsible and I wanted to make sure the boys knew that as well. "God didn't take him from us," I said. "It was bad people who did it, not God!" It might have worked for a few minutes or hours, but Tyler was full of questions and curiosity. I imagine he was trying to work things out, but it was so hard for me to talk about any of it. I tried to answer his questions as best I knew how, and I tried to stay strong, but it seemed like there was no end to his need to know. As I struggled with my own faith, I wasn't sure that I was giving him the right answers.

The day after Johnny was killed, the principal and teachers of Diamond Hill Elementary had come to my mom's to see Jeffrey and Tyler, and I was touched by that. I thought that the school did a good job, considering the situation. By the end of August, it was time for the boys to return to school and I was scared for them to go. Nothing like this had ever happened to children in our area and I didn't want my kids to feel different from their classmates. The principal asked me what I thought the teachers should say to the classes. I told them to tell the students not to treat Jeffrey and Tyler any differently than they had before. Tyler was a comical child and he was okay with being the center of attention, but Jeffrey never wanted attention, and he hated to be in the spotlight. He was the reason why I was forcing the issue of not treating my boys any differently than before. Jeffrey especially hated for people to feel sorry for him so, as he went back to school, it was important to me that the other kids try to act normally, so that Jeffrey could be comfortable.

The teachers counseled Jeffrey and Tyler's classmates on how to treat the boys when they came back to school. To my knowledge, the kids treated them the same, though some of them asked my boys questions.

Tyler had friends and got along with everybody, so he played with his friends at recess. At lunchtime, though, somebody asked him something about the murder and Tyler didn't feel like talking about it so he moved away from the other kids and sat by himself at the far end of the lunch table. He didn't want to be around anybody. He doesn't remember it as a big upset or anything, just that he didn't want to talk about it. After sitting alone for the first couple of days, Tyler moved back and started talking to the other kids again.

CHAPTER 11

CLUES

OUR FAMILY LEARNED to live life without Johnny while the investigation continued around us. Investigators recreated the blood splatter and tested gunshot residue. Officers gathered information.

Even though the state had cleaned up the scene, traces of blood and stains lingered in our laundry room behind the washer and dryer, up on the cabinets, and in the door frame around the back door. The investigators applied a dye stain that reacts with enzymes and proteins in blood to recreate the way the blood splattered and then they used those patterns to reconstruct the events of Johnny's death. Based on how the blood dripped or splattered as it flew, they could reconstruct scientific theories about what happened. There was a lot of criss-crossing in the patterns, and that indicated that the blood was spewing from an open wound in motion. That is how we knew that Johnny had fought so hard, even when he was so badly hurt. The blood stopped at the top step of the back porch. The investigators explained that the tiniest splatters of blood were from the greatest force—the bullets. Those tiny blood patterns were on the back door, the frame, and the hinges. It indicated that Johnny had chased them all the way outside, or at least to the doorway, when they shot him.

Using the gunshot residue testing, the investigators also were able to determine the path of the bullets. When a gun is fired, the metals in the gun and bullet create a cloud. The person firing the gun would have this residue on them for about six hours and, when the gun is fired, the residue also settles on other things nearby. From the entry angles of the bullets and the settling of the gunshot residue, the crime scene analysts determined that the gun was fired from the ground, below where Johnny was on the porch.

According the investigation report, the week after the murder, around the same time that the story appeared in our weekly newspaper, Otis Compton called the police chief and left a message that he wanted to talk to him. Recording the conversation, Chief Johnson called him back. Otis told him that he'd heard that his name had been mentioned in connection to the murder. Of course, people all over town were talking about the murder, but Otis's mom had a friend who frequently visited my parent's store, the S&S Party Shop. People were definitely talking about it there. Maybe that's how Otis learned that his name was connected to the case, or maybe that had something to do with him getting concerned about what the police knew. Since Otis did not have a drivers license, Johnson and a SLED investigator drove out to see Otis at his girlfriend's parents' house.

As soon as the officials arrived Angel, Otis' girlfriend, handed the chief a composition notebook, like a child's school book. It was already opened to a page with writing on it. When Chief Johnson looked at it later, he saw that the front of the notebook had schoolwork in it and some drawings. Then, looking further, he studied two pages in particular. On those pages, dates were listed from Thursday, August 5 to Friday, August 13, with corresponding information recounting what Otis had been doing each day. It was as if they had tried to create a fake diary as an alibi. Chief Johnson said he had never seen anything like it before in his career. For Monday, August 9, the notation read, "Didn't go anywhere. Fat Baby's funeral was going on."

While the chief was at the house Otis called his lawyer, Joe Smithdeal.

The two spoke on the phone for a few minutes. Otis handed the phone to Chief Johnson so that the lawyer could speak to the officer. Johnson told Smithdeal that he was going to bring Otis to the station for questioning. Smithdeal did not object.

Angel walked with the men to the car. In the backseat of the police car, she saw a jewelry box. The chief had put my sister's jewelry box, which looked almost exactly like the one that had been stolen from me, in his car. I had given it to the police earlier that day so that they could see what mine was like. When Angel saw the jewelry box in the back seat of the chief's car she refused to get in, saying that she didn't want to touch the box. Angel wouldn't get into the car until Chief Johnson put Sherri's jewelry box in his trunk. It was a big show, as if Angel thought the police were going to frame her for the robbery and murder.

At the station, Otis made a statement. He said that, on the day of the murder, he had gotten up that morning between ten and eleven and had cut the grass at Angel's parents' house. Her parents lived on Smith Street in Iva. Otis claimed that he finished cutting the grass sometime around 12:30 and then he, Angel, and her dad loaded up the riding lawn mower and went to his mother's residence on Indian Branch Road in Starr, about a five minute drive from Angel's parent's house. Otis said that he had stayed there, cutting grass all afternoon and into the evening. He said that his stepfather came home and that he helped him fix his lawn mower, and at one point he went to his sister's house, right up the street on Brown Road. After that, he said, he went back to his mother's where he stayed for the rest of the night. He said that he knew Johnny Hanna by the name of Fat Baby, and that he knew that he lived on Hilley Road. He described the home as a blue trailer.

When the officers mentioned that investigators were testing samples from the house for blood, hair, and fingerprints that could place him at the scene, Otis asked how there would be any of that if he had stayed in the car. The officers asked Otis if he was in the car. He must have realized his mistake, as he told the police to arrest him or take him home.

They took him home.

CHAPTER 12

THE MAN OF THE HOUSE

TYLER CONTINUED TO have frequent and terrible nightmares, and I started having dreams. I dreamed that Johnny and I weren't together and he never came to see the boys. I was upset with him—angry—that he had abandoned them, and in the dream I argued with him about it. I argued with him in the yard and I argued with him on the phone, and I even argued with him in court.

I dreamt the dream three or four times a week, roughly every other day, for months and months. Feeling angry that he had left the boys, I fought with him night after night, just as I had fought with him in the earliest years of Jeffrey's life, when I felt like Johnny had turned his back on us.

At some point, I realized that I felt abandoned by him—again—even though this time he didn't leave us. He was taken from us. Still, the dream felt like he had abandoned them. Over and over again, night after night, I dreamt it, so that I had to remind myself by day that Johnny would have stayed to take care of us and protect us, no matter what. He would never have left again. I had to work hard to conquer my feelings of abandonment, though I still do have that dream sometimes.

As we started to heal, I knew one thing: I was not going to abandon

Johnny. I had never lost anyone before, and I didn't know a lot about coping with grief, but I knew that I was going to honor Johnny and remember him for the rest of my life, and it was important to me that my boys did the same. I didn't want them to forget their daddy, and I intended to do all I could to help them remember him.

I realized that this was a contrast with how Johnny's family had handled their pain when they lost Blake, and I knew good and well that I would not let the same thing happen with Johnny's memory. So whenever I saw his parents, Marshall and Barbara, I always talked as though Johnny was still around. It's not like I was trying to pretend that he was still alive—I knew that he wasn't—but I talked about him in the present tense. Mind you, talking this way about Johnny was not always the first thing on my mind, but I really did not want them to feel like they couldn't or shouldn't talk about Johnny with me. I wanted them to talk about him, especially with Jeffrey and Tyler. It was really important to me that they saw that Johnny's name was not a forbidden word. I think I made Marshall and Barbara feel comfortable that way, because they did talk about Johnny with us. In fact, they actually talked about Blake more, too. I was glad for that.

Thanks to a good many family and friends, we survived. From the start, we had to completely rebuild our lives and even had to find a new home. We wouldn't ever have been able to start rebuilding our lives if it were not for our family and friends pitching in and helping us. When the police let us back into our house on Hilley Road we got our stuff and moved it out, but we didn't have any place to put it. Johnny and I had a utility building on our land on Hilley Road, so I had that moved to my parents' land since we were staying with them. I stored everything I owned in the utility building.

After a while, my parents offered to help me buy a new doublewide mobile home, which I could put on their land. As we started to think about what we wanted Jeffrey said, "Mama, whatever you do, don't get a house that looks just like the one we got." I wanted to honor that. It was really the only thing I cared about, for Jeffrey and Tyler. We looked and found a nice house that had a different layout from our old house.

When we moved into our new house, I kept Jeffrey's words in mind. I would make our new house look different. But, as I unpacked our stuff, I realized that part of me wanted to create some sense of normalcy, some continuity, at the same time.

My best friend, Gayle Brown, was unpacking pictures and helping me get set up. "Sheila, do you want this picture out?" she asked, holding up a photograph of Johnny and the boys.

"Yeah," I answered. "I want it out."

"What about this one?"

I said yes to every picture. We didn't have many framed pictures but we had many albums full of photos, and I needed to buy frames so that I could see pictures of Johnny everywhere. We set up the living room with the furniture and all these pictures placed everywhere, and then Gayle stopped and said something to me. "Sheila, you've got to make this house look different," she said. "You got to make it look different."

I didn't understand what she was talking about, but she didn't push it. We got the house pretty well set up and the boys and I had been living in it for a few days. Suddenly, it clicked. I realized that I had arranged all my furniture and set everything up the exact same way it was at the other house. I realized that I had wanted to make sure I fulfilled what Jeffrey wanted but, at the same time, I didn't want to lose all of it—all of the memories and comforts of our old house. I wanted things to be the same as before, even though I agreed with Jeffrey wholeheartedly. *You can't do this,* I finally realized. *You are torturing yourself and you're torturing your boys. You've got to make it different!* I rearranged the furniture again until nothing looked as it had on Hilley Road. It felt like a new house, with pictures of Johnny everywhere.

The bed was different, too. Johnny and I had been about to get a new bed anyway because I had a bad back and our waterbed was killing me. As soon as Johnny died, I knew that I couldn't use the bed that we had shared, so I didn't put the waterbed back up. Instead, I went and bought myself a new bed.

Jeffrey didn't want the washing machine and clothes dryer, either. He wanted me to get new ones, so I went and bought a new washer and dryer. I probably should have thought of that myself, but it was Jeffrey who was thinking like an adult—and talking like one, too.

Once we lost Johnny, Jeffrey stepped into the role of an adult in many ways. Though he was ten-years-old, I talked to him like an adult. I never said, "Jeffrey, you don't have to do this." I let him do it, let him be strong, responsible, and on top of things. I let him be like that because I felt that it would help him to know that he was needed.

Even today, Jeffrey feels a lot of emotion arise when he is in a helpless situation and I think that, when he feels that he is in control, it helps him to overcome his sadness. What he went through was pure helplessness and fear, so by being the one who is strong and who takes charge of things helps him to feel that he can overcome his situation and his feelings. He thrives on being in control, and that started when Johnny died. From that moment on, Jeffrey believed that it was his job to be the "man of the house" and to take care of Tyler and me. Despite his fear and grief, Jeffrey wanted to be the young man his father raised him to be—strong, stoic, reliable, and responsible.

So while the parent is supposed to set an example and be the strong one, that's not how it was after this happened to my family. I got my strength from my sons. When I saw them wake up each morning and go on with their lives that gave me the strength to wake up each morning and go on with mine. It wasn't a typical parent-child relationship. That role was reversed for a long time.

Still, I feel a little guilty that I didn't stop Jeffrey from assuming control in certain situations. I think that, if I had stopped it, maybe he would have been able to go back to being a kid. Maybe he would have had a childhood. But then, I toy with the fact and wonder if I had stopped it, then maybe Jeffrey would have felt the helplessness and been overwhelmed by it. Those feelings might have been too hard for him, and maybe we wouldn't have been able to overcome all that we've overcome. Sometimes, I wonder if I did it right, or if he would have been better if I'd handled it differently. But you can't go back, anyway, as much as I wish we could.

Tyler was a different story. While Jeffrey behaved like the strong, disciplined, and responsible side of Johnny, Tyler emulated the fun and gregarious side of him. And Tyler was built like Johnny, too—stocky and muscular—with the same face and Johnny's personality to go with it. He was definitely Fat Baby Junior.

One time, I took the boys over to see Marshall and Barbara, and Marshall's sister, who lived in a house just a hundred yards up the road. At one point, I could see tears welling up in Johnny's aunt's eyes. "He's just like his daddy," she said. "He's just like him. . ."

As the months went by, it didn't get any easier for us to understand the reason why Johnny was taken from us. Nothing seemed to make sense. I struggled a lot, thinking about that woman who had said that it was God's will. How could a God of all that is good want something so horrible? How could God want something to happen to a good man like Johnny? None of it made sense, and certainly not God. I just tried to understand that we don't get to be God and we don't always get to know God's reasons, so we just have to have trust that there is a reason. We have to have faith in Him, to work on trusting, and to learn to be okay with it. That's what faith is.

I just wasn't sure that I had it anymore.

CHAPTER 13

IN THE CROSSHAIRS

THE INVESTIGATORS WORKED to pin down a timeline for Otis's whereabouts on August 6. Agent Elizabeth Corley met with Otis's mom, who said that Otis was at her house from two o'clock in the afternoon until eleven o'clock the next night. She said he mowed her grass, ate dinner with her, and then mowed his sister's grass. When Corley asked her to write down her statement and sign it she hesitated, saying she didn't have her glasses. Corley offered to write it for her.

Corley began writing on the form titled Voluntary Statement. "I am Otis Compton's mother," she said. "I know he was at my house on Friday, August 6, 1999, from approximately two p.m until Saturday, August 7, 1999 until eleven p.m. He did not leave my house until Saturday."

Even then, Otis's mom seemed reluctant to put her signature on the statement, Corley would later recall, but she was adamant about one thing: her son was with her all that time. He never left her house.

But Otis's soon-to-be father-in-law drew a different timeline. Lieutenant Sandy Templeton met with Angel's dad on September 21. Her dad told Templeton that he and Otis had cut grass together at his house on the morning of August 6. The blade on his mower had broken, so he took it into town to be fixed while Otis charged the battery on the other mower and fixed the tire. They cut the grass, he said, and then had lunch. While they were in for lunch, Otis told his mom that he would come over and cut her grass, too. At around one o'clock, Angel's dad drove Otis and the mower over to Otis's mom's house. They dropped off the mower and then Angel's dad took Otis to his daughter's house. Angel's dad stayed for about twenty minutes. Though he could not remember exact times, he later said that he had left Otis at Angel's house sometime between 1:40 and 2:40 that afternoon. He did not see Otis again until around 8:30 or 9:00 that night, when Otis and his stepfather stopped by to get some cash that Otis had at the house. He said that he and his stepdad were going to the store to get cigarettes.

On November 30, Otis pled guilty to a number of other burglaries. He was sentenced to concurrent sentences of fifteen years. Since they were violent burglaries, Otis would have to serve eighty-five percent of his sentence before he would be eligible for parole. He was going to be locked up for more than twelve years.

He was not happy.

Detective Alford asked Agent Gambrell to help him escort Otis from the courtroom to the jail, across the street. As they walked, Otis struck up a conversation. He said that he had some information that might be helpful to him in the Johnny Hanna murder case.

Gambrell and Alford took Otis to the front office of the jail.

Otis told them that, on the day Johnny died, Johnny and I had gotten into a big argument about a dog that Johnny had bought. Otis said that he had heard this at the S & S Party Shop and that he had been hanging out there, trying to get information. He also said that, the night before the murder, I was working the 4:00 to midnight shift, while a black girl by the name of Julia was at our house from 10:00 p.m. until midnight. Otis said he didn't know what Julia was doing there. He also declined to disclose his source for this information.

I had worked the day shift that day. Of course, that was a simple matter to verify. It didn't matter to Otis. He was angry about his sentence, and possibly hoped to trade on information—bogus or not—in the murder case. He started naming names.

He asked Alford and Gambrell if the names Shane Rice or Robert Compton had come up in their investigation.

The officers took Otis to the Perry Correctional Institution in Spartanburg. He spent half a day there, being photographed and "dressed out" into his prisoner jumpsuit. Then, he was taken to Kirkland Reception and Evaluation in Columbia. He was there for twenty-two days while he was drug-tested, blood-tested, and underwent other tests. Finally, he was delivered to Kershaw Correctional Institute northwest of Columbia, where he would serve his sentence. He settled back into life as an inmate.

Otis had another burglary conviction that required sentencing, though, so in January the South Carolina Department of Corrections took him from Kershaw to the courthouse in Anderson County. They woke him up at six in the morning, shackled him, and put him on a bus. When he arrived at the courthouse, he was put in an eight-by-ten holding cell that had a concrete bench all around, along with a handful of other prisoners. There, he had a chance meeting with another prisoner, who would change everything.

Otis had another five years added on to his sentence, to be served concurrently.

CHAPTER 14

"FROM MAMA
AND DADDY"

A FEW TIMES a week, I continued to have the recurring dream about Johnny abandoning the boys. Eventually, it only came to me once a month or so. I felt like it would never leave me.

It was the same thing with the word "murder." I could not bring myself to say that Johnny was murdered. I would say that Johnny died in 1999. I could say he passed away. But I could not say "Johnny" and "murder" in the same sentence. It seemed to go on for the longest time—years, really—and I felt like I would never get over that.

That first Christmas, I felt like I needed to make it up to the boys that they didn't have their daddy. Since Christmas was Johnny's birthday, too, it was a rough day and I really went overboard with the gifts for them. The boys got a golf cart, clothes, shoes, video games, and toys. I think anybody would want to shower their kids with love and goodies to try and make up for what they are missing, but, of course, I could never make it up. There is no amount of giving that I could do. I could spoil them rotten forever and they still didn't have their daddy. I can't give them anything that could make it right for them, but, as the mama, it's what I needed to do. It helped me feel like I was at least doing something.

The thing that was really sort of off was that I signed every gift from "Mom & Dad." Before we open a gift, we always read who it is from, even still today. The boys were opening gifts and one said, "Okay, you have to read who it's from before you open it." So, before the other boy opened his gift, he read the card and said, "It's from Mama and Daddy."

My dad was there with us, and he looked at me. He thought the boys were just saying it and it bothered him. "Did you sign it like that?" he asked me.

I did. I really signed them that way. I only did it that year. I don't know why I did it.

That Christmas day was the first time that the boys and I felt safe enough to go to the cemetery and visit Johnny's grave by ourselves. The three of us sat on the gravel at the grave site, reminiscing about our other Christmas days. As we sat there talking, Tyler was digging in the gravel and I wasn't thinking anything about it. Then I noticed that he had dug-out a spot where the black plastic on top of the vault peeked through. I was angry. I asked Tyler why he did that. "I want to see my daddy," he said. My anger immediately turned to sorrow as I tried to explain to both of them that they won't see their daddy again until we go to Heaven. Tyler cried, and I held him close. It was too much heartbreak for me to try and hide my tears from the boys and as much as I tried to hide my weakness in front of them, I sat there with them that Christmas day and let my own tears flow.

We were all so focused on the boys after Johnny's death, trying to make up for their loss, but I saw that his death affected so many other people. All over town, there was a run on alarm systems, and everybody started locking their houses. People were scared as they realized that violent things— even murder—could happen in our little neck of the woods. Everyone was impacted.

Johnny's friends and our extended family suffered, too. My niece, Leanne, was really close to Johnny and, before he died, he had been babysitting her. She always had a bubbly kind of personality but, after he died, she changed. She became more quiet, serious. I think the murder had made her realize that life was not wonderful all the time. She was nine-years-old when Johnny died. Sherri, my sister, said, "Every time we'd get ready for bed Leanne would ask, 'Has the burglar alarm been set?'" She is still terrified, even now, and she later passed that on to her younger sister, Makayla, who is scared of her own shadow.

One thing that was nice to see, though, was how the community pulled together. For one thing, there was a fundraiser to help us raise money so that we could offer a reward for information about the murder. Though they asked that nobody tell me where it came from, I later found out that our Hilley Road neighbor, the nursery, made a large anonymous donation to help us. I thought that it was amazingly generous of them to do something like that.

Johnny's death brought our community together in other ways, too. However I can, I had to find the good in it. After the woman told me that it was "God's plan" that Johnny was murdered, I started skipping church. I did go talk to the preacher—I met with him a lot— and I told him about her comment. I said, "I hope you can explain that." He worked with me and helped me to see my way clear by reflecting back on the Bible and reminding me that God does not wish or bring bad things upon people. He is a loving God and He loved me and the boys and He made a promise to never forsake us.

I know it wasn't God's plan, but I believe God knew it was going to happen and He had a couple of reasons for allowing it. For one, I think something worse could have happened. I have no idea what could be worse, but, at the same time, I realized that the boys had stayed with Johnny through the whole summer and this just happened to be the first day of school. If the circumstances had been just slightly different, I could have lost my whole family.

I also think that Johnny has a testimony. I realized that his life could open up people's eyes to Him, and bring people to Christ's salvation. If Johnny's death meant that even one person was saved it was worth it, but many more were saved and brought into a personal relationship with God. I gave my testimony many times, though it was actually more Johnny's testimony. I tell people what happened to Johnny and how close his baptism was to August 6. I tell them about surviving. I talked about overcoming the worst circumstances you can imagine, and how you have to keep going. God is the one out front, the one who helped me through it. He was present in my life, and He's the one that gave me the will and the strength to keep going when I thought that I could not go on. To keep me going through all that I suffered, it had to be something really strong.

CHAPTER 15

LISTENING POST

AT ANDERSON COUNTY courthouse, shuffling in with his legs shackled, inmate Paul may have scanned the grey cell, checking out the other inmates who were waiting for yet another sentence to be handed down to them. Then Paul saw a familiar face he knew from growing up. Otis Compton.

I understand that convicts often discuss their charges, sentences, convictions. It's like the "So, what did you do?" conversation.

Paul reached out toward Otis's hand and they shook, pulling together for a quick neck hug. He told Otis some of his details and mentioned that he was doing his time at McCormick Correctional Institute. They settled in on the cold concrete bench and caught up, the stories of their unfortunate lives mostly relating to drugs and crimes.

Otis surprised Paul with his situation. He told him he was serving a fifteen-year sentence, taking the fall for some burglaries that his girlfriend, Angel, had committed. He told Paul that he needed Angel to keep quiet about a murder charge he was trying to avoid. According to Paul, Otis said was a burglary that "went bad" and he "did what had to be done."

Paul returned to McCormick and Otis returned to Kershaw, and they served their time.

In March officers on another, unrelated case questioned Paul to find out what he knew about their investigation. Paul let them know that he had more to share. While meeting with a SLED arson investigator, Paul mentioned that he had some information about the Johnny Hanna murder. He asked the investigator to have the sheriff call him. Sheriff Goodwin gathered the officers involved in the investigation, and they drove down to McCormick Correctional Institute.

Sheriff Goodwin, Detective Alford, Chief Johnson, and Lieutenant Templeton met with Paul around a sterile conference table at McCormick. Paul described his conversation with Otis. He told them that Otis said he was taking the fall on a burglary for his girlfriend because he wanted her to keep quiet about a murder. He told them that Otis had said that he had done what had to be done when a burglary went bad. Paul had an idea for the investigators. He proposed that they place him at Kershaw, with Otis, so he could listen and report back anything that Otis might say about the murder. It's my feeling that Paul opted to do this because he knew me and Johnny, and his mother went to our church.

The officers told him that they could not promise anything but that, if Paul did happen to end up at Kershaw, he should just listen. He should not ask any questions.

"You don't do a thing," Goodwin cautioned Paul. "Just be a listening post."

Johnny was my first love.

We were a happy family.

With his birthday on Christmas Day, Johnny was especially joyful on our favorite holiday of the year.

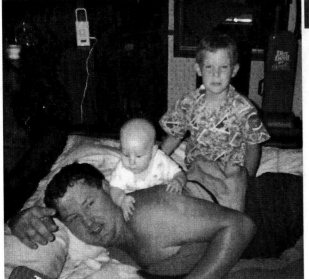

The boys enjoyed waking up their daddy.

Johnny was proud of his sons, Jeffrey and Tyler.

Three generations posed together, Johnny and his parents,
Marshall and Barbara, with Jeffrey and Tyler.

Johnny enjoyed hunting, and the boys looked up to their daddy.

Johnny's gun cabinet was ransacked the day of his murder.

One of the last good memories the boys have of that
summer was attending a Braves game at Turner Stadium.

Jeffrey was ten years old and Tyler was six when they came home from school and found their father murdered.

Here is where the boys loaded onto the bus to head home the afternoon of the first day of school.

The boys walked up this driveway. It would be their last moment of innocence.

The view from the kitchen, with light pouring
in from the laundry room where Johnny was murdered.

The laundry room
was covered in blood.

Johnny's body
lay across the door-
way, his legs on
the porch, holding
the door open.

Though we still own the house in which Johnny was
murdered, we no longer live there. It has since fallen into disrepair.

At their wedding,
Tosha and Jeffrey
honored both of their
fathers with flowers
and a memory table.

I am thrilled that
I gained a daughter.
Still, I missed
Johnny on our son's
special day.

It gives me joy seeing the wonderful husband
Jeffrey has become to his wife, Tosha.

Johnny's father, Marshall Hanna, provided support
and encouragement throughout the good times and bad.

I found love again with Keith Wiles,
my husband of eleven years.

I believe Johnny would have been proud of
the young men his sons have grown into.

CHAPTER 16

SNITCHES

WITHIN TWO WEEKS, Sheriff Goodwin arranged to have Paul transferred from McCormick Correctional Institute, near the Georgia border, to Kershaw Correctional Institute, way up near North Carolina.

Paul was placed in the north yard while Otis was in the south yard. The only interaction they had then was in the mess hall, where Otis was assigned to work. According to testimony, after he finished his job in the serving line, he would often come around to talk with the other inmates. Meals were a social time, and the inmates liked to joke around and show off. One day, a group of men—Paul as well as guys named Keith and Glenn, and another inmate—sat around a row of tables, perched on four stools. Otis dropped onto a stool at the next table. He laughed as he formed his thumb and finger into the shape of a gun, which he pointed at the men.

Pow. Pow. Pow. Pow. Otis pretended he was shooting. He repeated the phrase he'd used before—that he did what he had to do. Even when the other inmates expressed disbelief, Otis continued bragging. He even made a comment about what a big guy Johnny was. "I can't believe he said something like that," one of the inmates muttered after Otis left.

Before long Otis was moved to the north yard, where Paul was. They saw each other more, hanging out and sometimes playing handball in the courtyard. Otis's new roommate had only a few days left on his sentence, and, since Paul was in a three-man cell, the two talked and decided to see if they could be moved in together when Otis's roommate went home. The caseworker agreed.

Otis, Keith, and Paul often hung out in the courtyard, sitting around talking about old times. All three men were serving time for burglaries and, one day, their conversation turned to their crimes.

Otis said that he and Robert Compton had hit a double-wide to get some jewelry, guns, and cash to buy crack. He said that Shane Rice was in the truck, waiting for them, when someone walked in. He said it was a big guy and they couldn't take him. Again, he said, "I did what I had to do."

Paul took it all in and then reported the story back to Sheriff Goodwin.

Paul met with Goodwin in a meeting room at Kershaw Correctional Institute. Paul and Keith repeated Otis's story that he had been in the house when somebody walked in on them—a pretty good sized fellow. He tried to struggle with him, but the guy was too strong for him. So, one of them got a bat—he didn't say what kind—and started striking him. Then, they said, Otis told them that Robert Compton stabbed the guy, and part of the blade broke off inside of him. Otis said he shot him, too—four or five times, in the head and the chest. They reported that Otis had said that, for the final shot, he straddled the guy and just shot him in the head.

CHAPTER 17

A NEW YEAR

THE BOYS, ESPECIALLY at their ages, really needed a father. Johnny's cousin had been Johnny's hunting partner, and he stepped up for Jeffrey. He took him hunting and fishing and taught him a lot, but my dad really was the one who came through for the boys. They considered him their father figure. When Tyler was old enough, my dad took him hunting as well. Jeffrey spent most of his time with his "papa." They worked together on my parents' land, took care of the cows, and fished together. The boys practically lived with him.

The spring after Johnny died my dad decided to plant corn and beans in our field, just like Johnny had always done. The stalks were still out from the year before, so he needed to plow it first. He was out on the tractor, and a few of his friends were helping him, when he found a bag. Johnny had sold his old truck not long before he died, and I had just taken all the stuff out of it—his cassette tapes and other things—which I had put it in a plastic grocery bag that I stuck in his closet. The killers had taken it, but for some reason they dropped it out by the field, by that dirt track that ran around the edge of our land. For all those months, nobody had known about the bag, but Otis had mentioned it when he was questioned. We called the police and turned the bag over to them.

Other than hoping for justice, our healing wasn't moving forward much. And, of course, I remained primarily concerned for the boys and their well-being. At that point, I knew that counseling was probably a good idea. All three of us went to a woman named Miss Cherry. They don't remember much about it, other than playing games like Candyland. They said it was like she was a babysitter, so I don't know if it helped them. They did not want to talk about what had happened. Their lives were changed and there was nothing we could do about it. Though Jeffrey had always been on the Honor Roll at school, he never made the Honor Roll again after Johnny died. I think that he had checked out emotionally. As time went by, his grades dropped and since he didn't get in trouble for it he just kept slacking off.

I struggled with some really low points. There was one night in particular when I felt that the world was on my shoulders. It was probably the first time I felt like I couldn't take it anymore. I was wishing that it would have been me instead of Johnny who had walked into the house that day. Boys need their father to help guide them, show them how to do things, play ball with them. What did I have to offer?

I also blamed myself for what happened. If I had locked the door when I left, then it wouldn't have happened. If I had come straight home after the doctor's appointment instead of eating and shopping, it wouldn't have happened. If I had arranged the furniture differently, where no one could see the gun cabinet from a window, it wouldn't have happened. I convinced myself that it was my fault, and my thoughts were that the boys would think the same thing when they got older. Around this time is when I quit going to Miss Cherry for myself. I was afraid that someone might determine that, if I was in therapy or "seeing a psychiatrist," I must be an unfit mother who couldn't take care of her boys. I couldn't risk losing my boys, and I knew that there was a chance that could happen since I was not completely well, at least mentally. So I didn't go for long, though I recognize that it might have done me some good. At least I kept the boys going for a while.

What has helped me is prayer. Every week, at the end of our church service, anyone who wants or needs to can walk the aisle to talk to the preacher. I did it several times, asking him to please pray for me. Each time, he prayed for me right then.

I needed the prayers! There had been no arrest and rumors were flying rampant in our small town. Those rumors cut deep, and one of them really brought me down. My brother served in the National Guard and was in the process of moving to Tennessee, where his post was located, and because of his plans to move and because he was one of the last people to see Johnny alive, a rumor spread that my brother had something to do with Johnny's murder. I knew that this was ridiculous, but it hurt me that someone would say something like that about my brother. My brother and his wife stepped in and immediately offered support to the boys and me. He had helped us move our stuff from the old house. He had cried when the boys asked him questions about their dad, when he didn't know what to do to give them comfort. He had stepped up to give the boys another father figure. How could anyone make such an accusation about my brother, a man who was just like a brother to Johnny?

Another rumor went around that I had something to do with Johnny's murder. It bothered me that people could think that I was that type of person. How could someone think that I would do such a horrendous thing to my first true love, the man I wanted to spend the rest of my life with, the father of my boys? I shed many tears over this rumor. And, then, at some point, I got angry. I realized that my kids could hear this rumor someday, and it would cause them more pain. It made me angry, and it became my mission to prove that this was a lie. I told the Sheriff and Chief Deputy that I wanted to do a polygraph test, and I said that I wanted them to ask me anything and everything. I wanted them to get my fingerprints, verify my alibi, and do anything else they could do to stop the rumor before it reached my children. I had done most of these things already, however, and the police told me that no matter what I did people were going to talk and tell lies. I was stuck, wondering if I should talk to the boys about it before they heard something, or if it would be better not to mention it to avoid upsetting them and just hope they didn't hear it. I chose to be open. I sat the boys down and explained that people were saying some very mean things about me and other family members but that none of it was true. They wanted to know what kind of mean things people were saying. I didn't want to tell them, but I didn't want to lie to them either. I told them. I was sure they were going to ask a hundred questions but, instead, Jeffrey simply said, "That's stupid."

I worked with the police as the 911 Coordinator, and understood completely that the police needed to rule me out. I went to take a polygraph test. Still, it was hard. One of the questions that the examiner asked me was, "Did you murder Johnny Hanna?" I broke down, couldn't even answer. It didn't sound right to me to put the words "murder" and "Johnny" in the same sentence. It just didn't go together. It was hard enough to say that my husband had died, much less to say that he'd been murdered.

CHAPTER 18

UNDER PRESSURE

I THINK THAT Otis was in prison when he married Angel. In July of 2000, she was facing trial for her alleged role in the other burglaries and, as her husband, Otis was allowed to leave Kershaw to attend her trial, during which he was housed in the Abbeville County jail. Ever since he was sentenced, Otis had continued to look for ways to get his sentence reduced. In January, he filed for a post-conviction relief (PCR), a request for a review, arguing that his lawyer did not do his job well. Otis said later that he believed his lawyer did a good job, and he knew that he only had a year to file for a PCR and he didn't want to miss his opportunity. Otis was desperate for any opportunity to reduce his sentence. He said a few times that he wanted to beat his wife home.

Waiting in the county jail during Angel's trial, Otis told the jailer that he needed to talk to Sheriff Goodwin.

As was his routine, Goodwin walked into the jail that morning to pick up paperwork and to check in, and the jailer told him that Otis wanted to talk to him. Heading upstairs, Goodwin wondered what his number-one suspect might have on his mind.

Otis told Goodwin that he had some information that might be helpful in regard to the Hanna case. In return, he wanted his sentence reduced on the burglary charges—from violent to non-violent. A violent conviction requires that eighty-five percent of the time be served before the convict can be considered for parole. With a non-violent conviction, the sentence could be reduced to seven-and-a-half years, and Otis could be eligible for parole even sooner than that. He would likely have to serve only one-third of that time.

Goodwin gathered some of other officers on the case and asked Otis if he wanted a lawyer. Otis requested Joe Smithdeal, the lawyer who had represented him on the burglary charges. Templeton and Goodwin immediately took Otis to Smithdeal's office in Greenville, about an hour away. On Otis's request, they called Solicitor Townes Jones IV to join them there. As prosecutor, Jones had the authority to make plea bargains, and he was the prosecutor who gave Otis five years to run concurrent for the third burglary charge.

By the time they were all together and working on the agreement, it was Friday night. Goodwin recited the Miranda rights to Otis and handed him a written copy of his rights. "You have the right to remain silent. Anything you say can and will be used against you in a court of law. You have the right to talk with a lawyer for advice before we ask you any questions and to have him or her present with you during questioning. If you have no money for the lawyer's fees, the Court will appoint one to represent you without cost to you, if you wish. If you decide to answer questions now without a lawyer present, you still have the right to stop answering questions at any time. You also have the right to stop answering questions at any time until you talk to a lawyer. I have read this statement of my rights and understand what my rights are."

Otis signed the document.

Then, they presented him with a waiver of rights. "I'm willing to make a statement and answer questions. I do not want a lawyer at this time. I understand and know what I am doing. No promises or threats have been made to me and no pressure or coercion of any kind have been used against me."

Gambrell filled out the top part and slid it across to Otis and Smithdeal. They read it and they signed it.

Then they used a legal boilerplate to work out the terms of the plea bargain. The agreement would become "null and void," it stated, "if the State determined that Otis had been untruthful in any representations made to the state concerning the murder and death of Johnny Hanna." The state agreed to reduce the sentences "by all reasonable means on the indictments to burglary second degree nonviolent, with a sentence of seven and one-half years to run concurrent with all other sentences Otis was now serving or would be serving within eighteen months of arrest or within two years from the date of this agreement."

The officers made sure that Otis was comfortable and assured him that it would be a clear case if he cooperated fully and truthfully about his knowledge of the Johnny Hanna murder case.

Otis wiped his hands on his prisoner orange pants and situated himself in his chair. Then he told his tale.

He said that he, Shane Rice, and Robert Compton had gone out drinking and smoking drugs. He said he and Shane took Robert home, and then went to ride around some more and drink some more beer. After they rode around a while, Otis said, they went to a hangout on a country road called Doc's Kitchen, where Shane told him what happened at the murder. Otis told the police that Shane had said that he and Robert went to the Hanna's house to burglarize it. While they were there, Otis said Shane told him, Johnny came home and surprised them. Otis said that Shane told him that Robert had stabbed Johnny and that he had shot Johnny several times.

The statement was written. Otis signed the top and Smithdeal signed the bottom.

CHAPTER 19

MEMORIAL

ON THE FIRST anniversary of Johnny's death, I organized a memorial service for him. We played some of the songs that we had used at his funeral. I got up and told the story about our honeymoon—how I called down to the valet for him to bring up our Cadillac, when we were actually in Johnny's old beater truck. Everybody laughed. They could picture Johnny driving around in that old truck that he had for so long. It was good for us to all remember him that way—strong and alive.

My friend, Jeff Collier, is like a singing preacher, the kind who is loud and hyper. He'd jump up on the pew and make sure he had everyone's attention. He lived in North Carolina and performed across the South and, sometimes, he'd come back to our church. He was not able to perform at Johnny's funeral, though we did play some of his songs on CD. He asked me if he could sing at the memorial service and I was thrilled. He sang one of the songs that we had played at the funeral, and it really got to me. It always gets me teary-eyed.

Before Jeff started singing, he talked about surviving. We are still here, he said, and we have to live our lives. The boys needed a daddy—and made no secret that they wanted one desperately—but Jeff explained that they have a daddy, our Heavenly Father. He had written a song, which he dedicated to my boys, telling them, "You may grow up without your earthly father, but you have a father that will be right at your side for the rest of your life. He knows the pain and suffering you are going through and He will carry you through it. Just learn to lean on Him."

Jeff had written the song about his own life growing up without a father, and had called me to tell me about it. "Sheila, I want to sing you the chorus," he had said. "I wrote it because of my own life, but after I read through it, I want Jeffrey and Tyler to hear this song." He sang the chorus over the phone to me, and I was so touched by it. It really hit home. Soon after he told me about the song, Jeff recorded it. The boys and I were sitting in the congregation when he sang the song. First, he went up to the front of the church and looked at us. "Jeffrey and Tyler," he said, "this is for you."

I know without a doubt that God was there, holding our hands as Jeff Collier sang this song:

"The Father You Never Had"

In '62 came a son to this ol' troubled world
Just a babe born with a cross to bear
and soon he'd learn that the hand that life had dealt was hard and cruel
without a dad or mom, what a grandma had to do

The lad grew up into a man to face the world alone
A broken heart, a battered mind, what a lonely soul
Running scared to the end that he'd surely face
Till he heard Heaven's voice gently say

I'll be the Father you never had
And I'll be there thru the good times and all the bad
And in life's games, I'll stand and cheer when it's your turn to bat

Oh I'd be glad to be the Father you never had.

If this song sings to you a melody of truth
And your future is haunted by a painful past
There is one at the door with His arms open wide and He longs just to be
your Dad

He'll be the Father you never had
And I know He'll be there thru the good times and all the bad
And in life's games, He'll stand and cheer when it's your turn to bat

Oh, He'd be glad to be the Father you never had.

CHAPTER 20

CONFESSION

I N A GRAY CELL in Columbia, on the evening of October 9, 2000, Otis and Paul had summoned a ride, and then they waited. Otis claimed that, the night before, Paul had advised him to place himself at the scene. Then he'd "be a free man," Otis said he was told. The two then told an investigator at Kershaw to let Sheriff Goodwin know that Otis wanted to talk. The Abbeville County officers agreed to pick them up in Columbia, halfway between Kershaw and the Abbeville County Courthouse.

Lieutenants Gambrell and Templeton drove separately and picked up Otis and Paul. Templeton read Otis his rights, and they drove the two hours from Columbia to Abbeville. Otis rode with Gambrell; Paul went with Templeton.

Chief Johnson and Sheriff Goodwin joined the lieutenants and the felons in a conference room set up with snacks and drinks. Johnson took the handcuffed Otis out the back steps of the courthouse, handed him a cigarette, and lit it for him.

"Just tell the truth here," Johnson said. "You have to tell the truth."

Back around the conference table, littered with pictures from the crime scene, Otis opened up. He said he ran into Shane Rice and Robert Compton at Crescent Grocery when he was buying cigarettes. They talked for a while, got into Rice's truck, and left the store. They rode around for a while, down Highway 81 and Mount Vernon Church Road. They smoked some crack, and either Otis or Robert brought up a place they had been casing, where there were guns and stuff they could steal to get money for some crack. Nobody was supposed to be home until after five o'clock.

He said they went to the rear of the house and tried to kick in the back door and pry it open, but they couldn't get in. One of them checked another door and got into the house and came around and opened the back door for them. Otis claimed he stayed outside and that Rice and Compton went in. He said he heard a racket of some sort, looked up, and saw that the owner had come in. He told the officers that there was a fight in the house.

Otis told the officers that the men stumbled out the back door and he saw Robert stab Johnny in the chest and Rice hit him with a bat. Then, Otis explained, he saw Rice shoot Johnny in the arm and in the stomach and then in the head. He said the knife was still in Johnny, and the bat was on the bed.

Otis ran off into a field with three bags of stuff. Rice jumped in the truck with him, he said, and he sped off. He said they had a wallet with $700 in it, and he took $200 out for himself. Then they threw the wallet out at the intersection of North Road and Highway 81. Then he went to his mom's house. He said that he didn't talk to anybody, just started cutting the grass like nothing happened. Rice and Robert, he said, went to see their drug dealer to buy more crack. After he finished his confession, Otis said he was tired and wanted to go lie down.

The next day, the officers took him out to our house, to the crime scene.

Dr. Woodard the pathologist who did Johnny's autopsy, Steve Derrick from the forensics lab, Detectives Alford, Gambrell, and Templeton all met at our house to walk through the scene of the murder with Otis. Otis asked if Paul could come with them and the Sheriff allowed it.

On the trunk of the patrol car in the driveway, Alford filled in another form with Otis's Miranda rights again. He asked Otis to sign it.

"I don't want to sign any more forms," Otis scoffed.

Alford noted on the form that Otis stated he understood his rights, did not want to sign anything, but still wished to answer questions.

Otis walked ahead, leading the officers to the back of the house.

"That's the pole I almost hit," he said, pointing to a telephone pole with a light mounted on it.

Otis stepped onto the deck and continued to narrate the story of the horrible day. He said that he was standing behind the house after Robert and Shane had gone in. They were bringing stuff out, stacking it up by the back door. He said he then took some of the items from there to the truck. He said that, while he was standing in the backyard, he thought he heard a vehicle arrive. He said he looked around over the pool deck and saw Johnny's black pick-up pull up and park underneath a tree. He said he didn't really know what was going to happen. He hoped those guys got out of there quickly. He said about a minute or so later he heard a commotion inside. He said a window broke near the left of the back door and he saw Robert come running toward the back of the house and hiding behind a door. He said Johnny came out through the back door and Robert jabbed him underhand in the neck and in the chest area with a knife. He said they then got into a big struggle and fell to the floor, grabbing each other.

He said that, while they were on the floor, Shane came through, jumping over them, onto the porch and down the stairs into the yard. He said Robert then jumped up off the floor, ran outside, and put his hand on the porch rail to vault over it onto the grass. He said Robert took off running toward the field and that, as soon as Robert started running, Otis started the vehicle, ready to go, when he heard shots.

Shane started shooting, he said. The first bullet Shane shot hit Johnny in the arm with the watch on it. He then said that, with the second shot, Shane shot Johnny in the stomach area, which knocked him to the porch. He said Johnny was basically on the top step of the porch, and as the shot hit him, he fell backward. He said immediately after that, he heard two more shots. He said Shane had one foot on the bottom step and one on the ground and he shot two more times, striking Johnny. He said Shane then went up the steps, straddled Johnny, stood over him, and shot one time straight down into his head. He said that Shane came back down and got into the truck with him. He said they drove away in a hurry, digging out in the grass and almost hitting the pole. He said they drove down the dirt track and took a right on Hilley Road to where the pavement ended. Robert came up and jumped in the back of the truck and they kept going down Hilley Road. At some point, they stopped and Robert got out of the back of the truck and got into the cab with them. Robert was counting the money in the wallet and dividing it up to three people, and they turned right on Highway 81 and went north, toward Iva, and that's when Robert threw the wallet out of the window of the vehicle.

Again, Otis said he drove back to Crescent Grocery, got out of the car, and went back to his mother's house. He stated that, when he got back, he didn't talk to anybody. He started cutting grass just like nothing happened.

The officers had a few questions to clarify Otis's story.

"Otis, these tracks dug out here, there's no way they were made by a truck," Templeton pointed out. "The wheel base is too small. These tracks were made by a small car."

Otis didn't respond.

"Now Otis, the bat you mentioned last night that Shane hit Johnny with," Alford asked. "Where was it?"

"He throwed it on the bed," Otis answered.

Alford and Templeton looked at each other and into the house from the deck. There was no way that Otis would have been able to see into the bedroom or onto the bed if he was sitting inside the truck.

CHAPTER 21

STRUGGLES

I HAD HEARD Keith Wiles's name mentioned, but I don't believe I met him until about a year before Johnny died. He was previously married to Darlene, Sherri's husband's sister. After Keith's divorce from Darlene, he remained close friends with Sherri and Doug. My family grew up playing all kinds of card games, and we spent many days and nights playing, but one game we started playing a lot was Hand and Foot. Not many people knew how to play the game back then except for a few of us, including Keith. Once or twice a month, my family would play cards at Sherri and Doug's house or at my parent's house. Johnny never did learn how to play. He tried a couple of times, but he didn't really care for it. The boys and I would usually go over to whoever's house to play cards while Johnny stayed behind or went to work. Keith occasionally would come over and play cards, too, and we met playing cards at my sister's house in the summer of 1998. Keith and I really never talked to each other unless it was about the card game. I am very competitive, so Keith and the rest of the family would joke about me getting mad if I lost. Of course, I really didn't!

Amazingly, Johnny met Keith on our vacation at the beach just weeks before he died. I was walking through the hotel parking lot with Johnny and the boys trailing behind me when I heard someone calling my name. It was Keith. I was able to introduce him to Johnny then. I really think God had a part in that.

When Johnny died and the boys and I were staying at my parents' house, the air conditioner couldn't keep the house cooled with all the people that were in and out. Keith helped Doug to install a window air conditioner. While they were putting the unit into the window, Keith came up to me and told me he was very sorry for what happened. I later found out that Doug had mentioned to Keith about how hot it was in the house and Keith told him he had an extra AC unit that they could put in at my parents' house.

I didn't see Keith again for a few months. The first two or three months after Johnny's death, I slipped into a depression. I did not think my depression was visible to other people. I went back to work one week after Johnny died. I was truly trying to stay focused and busy to not let the depression take over. My life for those first few months was work, home, and whatever the boys had going on at the time, whether it was sports or school related. Around the middle of November 1999, three months after Johnny's death, Keith went to the S&S to sing karaoke. He is not much of a drinker, but he likes to sing karaoke. I am the same; not too much a drinker, but I like karaoke. Apparently, Mama was worried about me not getting out and doing anything and put Keith up to calling and inviting me to sing one night.

I agreed, and it was the first time I was out in public after Johnny's death. Although the bar was full of people that I knew all my life, I felt out of place. People were hugging me and trying to make me feel comfortable. Eventually, I began to enjoy the night, singing karaoke and being around friends. Several hours later, Keith and I were the only two people left singing karaoke, and I caught myself laughing and having a good time. Immediately, I told Keith I had to go home. I felt guilty for having a good time, guilty that I was singing with another man—not that Johnny would ever sing karaoke—and guilty that I was not with my boys. I left the bar that night feeling like I was the worst person ever.

On Thanksgiving night, we played cards at Sherri and Doug's. My tradition is to go shopping the day after Thanksgiving. I always went by myself because Johnny said he wouldn't fight that type of crowd to save a couple of dollars. He just didn't understand. I mentioned during the card game that I wanted to go shopping the next morning but I didn't want to go by myself. I don't know if it was because I was scared, lonely, or a mixture of both, because I had never felt that way before. Everyone else grumbled that they had plans or didn't want to fight the crowd, but Keith spoke up. He would go with me, he said. Though I was happy to have a shopping partner, I was worried we might be getting closer than I was ready for.

Nevertheless, we went shopping the next day and had a great time. I think Keith was surprised by all the stuff I was buying the boys for Christmas. Of course, later that night, the guilt of being alone with him started getting to me.

After that, Keith became my confidant—someone I could talk to about my fears, my anger, and whatever other emotion that I was feeling. He was a great listener, exactly what I needed at the time to help me keep my sanity. Keith was working a swing shift, where he'd switch from first, second, and third shift every two weeks. He knew that I was scared for me and the boys, and he offered to stay with us at night when he was working first and second shifts. He also offered to keep his Jeep parked in our driveway all the time, to help ease our anxiety. It helped me feel protected.

Needless to say, since it appeared that Keith was staying with us all the time, rumors started again. I felt like I had to protect Keith, and I believe this is when I truly started to fall in love with him. I remember one day when we were talking, I told him that I was so very sorry that his name and reputation was being dragged in the mud because of me and that I would completely understand if he wanted to walk away from it all. His response was, "I don't care what they say about me. I care about you and the boys and I am not going anywhere."

I knew that I loved Keith, but I struggled with wondering if I loved him because he just happened to be the person that I was close to at the time or if it was true love. And as good as Keith was to the boys, Jeffrey had a hard time accepting him at first. Jeffrey made sure that Keith and I both knew that Keith was not and would not ever be his daddy. Jeffrey had some resentment toward Keith because he looked at him as someone who may one day "replace" his dad. On the other hand, Tyler became very close to Keith and often wanted to do things with him. My mind was so mixed up during this time. I didn't know if continuing to see Keith was the best thing for me and the boys. I later decided that it was unwise, so I told Keith that we couldn't see each other anymore. I said that I had a lot of baggage that he wouldn't understand. I knew I hurt him very badly. The next several days were like a blur. My body functioned, but my mind was shut down.

During this time, I had come home from work one day and my cousin, who was babysitting the boys for me, told me that something was wrong with Jeffrey. He wouldn't let her in his bedroom and she knew that he was crying. I went to his bedroom and he let me in. Immediately, I noticed that he was playing Vince Gill's song, "Go Rest High On the Mountain," the same song that we played at Johnny's funeral. Jeffrey was crying uncontrollably, and this was the first time that I saw Jeffrey truly cry after Johnny died. I later found out that he didn't want to cry in front of me or Tyler because he felt he would let his daddy down if he didn't take over as "man of the house," the strong one. My first instinct was to remove whatever it was that was causing him this pain, so I went to turn the radio off. Jeffrey said, "No, I want to hear it." I sat down on the floor with him and wrapped him in my arms as we cried together.

That night, drowning in my own self-pity and feeling like my boys would be better off without me, I needed to talk to someone who wouldn't judge me or tell me what a horrible mother I was for having suicidal thoughts. My first thought was to call my mom and dad, but I decided against that because they were already worried about me and I didn't want to cause them more worry. As much as I tried to talk myself out of it, I picked up the phone and called Keith. I didn't know if he would talk to me or hang up the phone. He answered the phone and I think I may have said something like "I need someone to talk to, but if you don't want to, I understand." We talked for about thirty minutes, and then he came over and we talked until the wee hours of the morning. My focus from the time Johnny died had always been on my boys, protecting them and giving them everything I could to help ease their pain. That focus was my saving grace many times. This time, though, I lost my focus—but Keith was there to put me back on track and save me. Needless to say, we were back together and I visited him the next week while he was on a fishing trip in Santee Cooper. Keith advised me not to bring the boys because the waters were too dangerous. Even then, he was looking out for them.

The best spiritual food for me during those days was leading the Youth Group. Johnny and I had started working with the youth right after we were saved that summer. I continued volunteering even after Johnny's death. These young people were hungry for the Word and would question each and every thing I said. They kept me on my toes and, more importantly, in the Word. Some of the members of the Youth Group later came up to me and said that they appreciated everything I taught them, but what they don't know is that they taught me. With their inquisitive minds, they forced me to open my heart and mind to God's Word again.

One evening in late spring of 2000, I was sitting at home when two men from the church knocked on the door. I invited them in, and they immediately told me that they didn't think it was right for me to be the Youth Leader while I was living with a man. I was flabbergasted. I asked them what they meant by "living with a man." One man said that he knew Keith was staying with us because he had seen him outside doing things and his Jeep was always here. Instead of explaining how Keith was there to offer us protection and comfort and telling them that Keith and I were not living together in that sense, I just asked them what they wanted to do. One man answered, "We are removing you as the Youth Leader, effective immediately." I told them that was fine and asked them to leave. I couldn't hold back the tears. I called Keith and told him what had happened. I told him I couldn't go back to that church. In reality, I was taking my anger out on the church as a whole instead of just those two men. I would find out later that the rest of the church members did not agree with those two men. Looking back, I should have confronted the other church leaders about this to find out what was really said, and then I would never have left that church. I later found out that the pastor did not agree with the deacons. He felt they made the wrong decision and considered leaving the church because he did not want to appear supportive of their position.

In the midst of it, I slipped back to blaming God for everything that was happening. But somewhere, Johnny's voice rose above my blaming game with the words "My boys will be raised in church." Then, I was on the search for a new church. Keith recommended the church he grew up going to, and it was the same church that my aunt attended. We started going to that church around the end of May—Vacation Bible School time. I was asked to help with the games and recreation, which I did. After VBS, my aunt asked me if I would consider helping with TeamKids, the class for kids ten and younger. I was hesitant but agreed to help, not lead. Once again, I found myself enjoying church again. The boys were active in church activities, so everything was going great.

I remember the day I heard about the arrests—Otis Compton and Robert Compton were arrested in October of 2000. It was a Wednesday night, and the boys and I were at church. I had about thirty kids in TeamKids that night, and my mom walked in. Now, my mom does not regularly attend church and most of the time only comes when we ask her or when something big is going on with her grandkids. When she walked through the door, I thought, *Oh my God! Something awful must have happened!*

She came up to me and said, "Sheila, the sheriff and chief are going to meet you at the party store in thirty minutes. They made an arrest."

The whole church could hear me holler! Those little kids looked at me

156

like I had lost my mind. Tyler was in that class and the kids kept asking him, "What's wrong with your mama?" After we left my aunt, who was also teaching that group, told me the kids wanted to know what was going on. She didn't want to tell them too much or give them more details than their young minds needed, so she told them that I had some good news about something that happened to Tyler's daddy. Of course, when we went to church the next time, all the kids asked Tyler, "What happened to your daddy?" Tyler handled it well and just answered, "My daddy died."

I knew that Jeffrey would run into Otis's daughter, Joy, at school the next day, so I told him, "Don't say anything to Joy." I explained to him that it wasn't her fault. It was her dad. I knew Jeffrey would handle it well. I had just walked into work when the school called for me to come pick Jeffrey up because he had been fighting. When I got there, I found out he was not really involved. Joy mouthed off a little to him, and his friends started mouthing off back at her. Joy's mom had already picked her up and taken her home. The school really worked with them and didn't put the kids in the same classes after that. They still rode on the same bus together, but there were no problems.

Before the murder, we knew these other families. We weren't best friends, but we were very cordial and always spoke when seeing each other. Johnny knew them, too. Ours is a small community, so our paths crossed often.

The third suspect, Shane Rice, was arrested a couple of days later. After they made the arrest, I was getting gas at a local store and Shane's dad, whom I knew from a previous job, pulled up next to me at the tank. "Sheila, can I talk to you for a minute?" he asked.

"Yeah," I replied.

"You know, Shane didn't do that," he told me.

I could not hear it. "I don't want to talk about it," I said. "In my opinion, he did do it and from what I've seen, he did it."

"Sheila, he really didn't," he stressed. "Will you listen to my side of the story?"

157

"I don't want to hear your side of the story," I said. And that was the end of it.

Many times I have thought about the families of these men. I tried very hard to understand their side and put myself in their shoes. They were hurting too and I didn't want to forget that, but at the same time, I wanted justice for Johnny. Robert posted bail and got out of jail on June 4, 2001, but there were stipulations that he was not to come within a hundred feet of me or the boys.

Soon after he got out, we were in WalMart shopping and I saw Robert and his girlfriend. I grabbed the boys, and went to the counter. "Do you know you have a murderer in your store?" I asked the cashier. Dumbfounded, she just looked at me. I don't know what possessed me to say that—anger, maybe, or just stupidity. I called the sheriff to tell him that Robert was in the same store as the boys and me. I thought he would have to leave the store. The sheriff explained to me that, since it was a public area, that if I saw him first I had to be the one to back away. I have not seen Robert since. I don't even know if he is still in South Carolina. I have never known his family, either, so I don't run into anybody else.

Johnny's mom, Barbara, could not handle the constant reminders, I guess. After the second anniversary of Johnny's death on August 25, 2001, she was overcome with grief and took her own life in her backyard. Jan Johnson, the paramedic who had come to my house, also responded to the call at Marshall's house that day, and still deals with the sadness of realizing that Barbara had taken her life. It was hard for everyone.

I have to admit that there were times when I considered it myself. There were days that I spent thinking, *I can't go home. I can't go on.* But I had to think of the boys, and that snapped me back to reality.

As a 911 telecommunicator, I dealt with suicide callers and I always thought of suicide as such a selfish act. When you are thinking of suicide, you are not thinking about the people close to you or how much they love you and what you would be putting them through. I could not end my own suffering without creating more suffering for my boys. If I killed myself, the boys would be orphans. My strength came from God, and my strength came from my boys.

I had to let the boys sort out their faith on their own. Tyler wanted to talk about Johnny all the time and Jeffrey kept it all inside. They fought. Eventually, they worked out their relationship with each other, and eventually they worked out their relationship with God. Tyler, in his question-asking phase, asked me "Why did God take Daddy?" Troubled by his question, I told him, "God did not do this! Do not blame God!"

But he did, at the beginning. Through my constant reminder and his own revelation, he realized that it isn't God's fault. God has a plan for everything, and eventually Tyler came to terms with that.

I struggled at work, too. In my job, I experienced stress on a daily basis. The work requires us to listen and respond to people's problems and traumatic events constantly. Once we send emergency responders to the scene we rarely hear the outcome, and that, by itself, is very stressful. Since I worked in a small 911 center, I didn't experience the very high stress level that most 911 telecommunicators experience in larger centers, but it's still a stressful job.

Before Johnny was murdered, I loved my job and everything about it. I loved being able to help anyone, even strangers. But then, when my husband needed my help, I wasn't able to help him. In a way, I looked at it as being hypocritical when I went back to work. Here I was, helping strangers with their emergencies but I couldn't help the one person that I loved the most.

It is common for 911 telecommunicators to experience Post Traumatic Stress Disorder (PTSD) after handling a traumatic call, such as a child not breathing or a shooting incident. But when it comes to 911 telecommunicators, PTSD is often overlooked because people think that, since we were not on the scene and didn't see the victims, we wouldn't have experienced the stress. This is far from the truth. We live with the horror and fear of wondering if we did everything we could to make a difference. Often, we will tend to use the "If" standard: "If I had done this or that, would it have turned out better?"

I knew that Christi and Keisha, the other women at the 911 Center the day it happened, would experience these feelings after taking Jeffrey's call and working with the responders that day. But I was experiencing my own PTSD and realized that I couldn't help them with theirs. Whether it was fear of finding out things that I didn't want to know—like what Jeffrey said on the phone—or just trying to get things back to normal, I never discussed what happened with the people I worked with.

Unfortunately, that is often the way it is in this business. We dig deep down, try to come to terms with what occurred, and go back to work the next day as though nothing is wrong. In 1999, most 911 centers did not offer their employees any type of counseling or debriefing to help them overcome these feelings. We have found that, over the years, it begins to eat away at you. Now, in 2013, only a few centers offer this service to their 911 telecommunicators. Now that I know how PTSD feels, I think it is a shame that all 911 centers don't offer this to the telecommunicators. This is the most rewarding job anyone could have, but not everyone can do it.

It took me a couple of months after Johnny died before I would actually go and sit down at the dispatch console at our 911 Center. I feared that I would answer a 911 call from a child who had discovered a parent not breathing. I wasn't sure I could handle that type of call without breaking down. My job at the time was to oversee the day-to-day operations and training, so I wasn't required to answer 911 calls unless the dispatch center got busy. At that point, when I would go to work and answer 911 calls, I would compare the caller's emergency to what was happening in my own life. I didn't ever do that before. Most people call 911 only once in their lifetime, and it is that one time when they are experiencing the most traumatic event ever. We are taught as 911 telecommunicators that we must be empathetic to the caller's situation. That is common sense. If you can't be empathetic then you don't need to be a 911 telecommunicator. People depend on you to help them through their problem. The importance of my job was diminishing in my mind because I felt that no one could experience more trauma than what the boys and I had experienced. My job went from being something I loved to do to something I had to do to get a paycheck and make a living. In this profession, you can't swing that type of attitude and get by with it. I was tired of listening to everyone else's problems at the other end of the phone line, when I had my own to deal with at home. I remember taking a 911 call from an elderly woman who woke up to find her husband had passed away during the night. Through her tears, she was telling me that they had just celebrated their sixtieth wedding anniversary a week before. Instead of putting myself in her shoes and realizing the pain she was going through from losing someone she had spent a lifetime with, my thoughts were "at least you had sixty years to be married to your husband. I only had seven years."

I never doubted my God-given talent to do this job until I went back to work after Johnny died. The breaking point for me was when I answered the non-emergency phone line and the caller stated, "I need to speak with the sheriff because I have some information about the Johnny Hanna murder case." Our policy was to transfer those type of calls directly to the Sheriff's Office, and I was in a position that I was responsible for making sure that everyone followed policy and procedure. But this time, I contemplated, "Should I transfer the caller or should I ask him what type of information he has?" I must have been contemplating a little too long because the caller spoke up and said, "Ma'am are you transferring me?" Without hesitation, I transferred him to the Sheriff's Office. I got up out of the chair and walked to the director's office and said, "I can't do this anymore. I have lost the passion and I can't hide or forget about my own problems to help other people with theirs." He said he understood and that he was going to call me in his office to talk to me about it anyway, because an employee had sent him an email that stated, "Sheila is not doing what she is supposed to be doing. I know she experienced a terrible time in her life but it has been months and she should be over it by now."

I thought be over it by now? Is there a time limit on how long it takes to go from losing everything you ever knew to regaining a normal life and attitude? My bitterness grew from that point. I started feeling like everyone could be saying things like that, and who were they to know how I felt? I wanted to scream out to everyone, "Let me put this in perspective so everyone can see how I got where I am in my life! My husband was murdered and no arrest has been made. I was left as the main caregiver of our boys, financially and mentally. We lost our home. We are scared to walk outside by ourselves and, when we do, we are constantly looking over our shoulder, and I am questioning my relationship with Christ. I don't want your pity or assumptions, but I will take your prayers." That is what I wanted to tell everyone.

CHAPTER 22

FATHER FIGURE

BEFORE KEITH AND I married, I asked Jeffrey if he thought his daddy would want me to get married again. He told me no. I was shocked, and I told him that I thought his daddy would want me to get married again. I knew he liked and respected Keith, though. Now that he's older, he tells me that he knows that his daddy would have wanted me to get married again, but he took my question literally. He was telling me what Johnny would have wanted if he still was alive.

On January 13, 2001, Keith and I married and I became Sheila Hanna-Wiles. Keith had a hard time at first, accepting that I didn't drop the Hanna name, but I tried to make him understand. I did it partly for the boys. I wanted us to have the same last name. It would help with signing papers for school to have the Hanna name in mine, just like theirs. But the main reason I didn't want to drop the Hanna was out of respect for Johnny. I did not want a new identity. I did not want for Keith and me to become a family separate from the boys. We are still a family, missing one person, but still a family.

We had a lot to work through in our marriage. All married people do, but Keith had to learn, in a way, to live with a ghost. He went with me to the cemetery one day, for his first time, and saw the headstones.

"Sheila, why did you have your name put on it?" he asked me.

"Because that is where I'm going to be buried," I told him.

"You're not going to be buried with me?" he questioned.

I explained that I just did not think that it would be right for the boys' daddy to be buried one place and their mama somewhere else. They would have to go to two different cemeteries to visit. And it didn't make any sense for Johnny to be buried there in my mom and dad's plot without me there. When we buried Johnny, I had no intention of remarrying; I was going through the motions and could not think about the future. I understood that this hurt Keith, but I did not know how to make it better.

It's still a struggle, but Keith accepted it. He told me that he wants to be cremated and have his ashes spread out over the lakes at Santee Cooper, his favorite pastime location.

Still, his jealousy was real. When we first got married, I had pictures of Johnny and the boys and our family portrait in the living room. Keith came to me. "Sheila, I am not asking you to take the pictures down completely," he said, "but can you move them to the boys' bedroom? Just think how you would feel if I had a picture of my ex up here?"

I got defensive about that very quickly. "Let me tell you something!" I shot back. "There is a difference in that you and your ex-wife quit loving each other. Johnny and I didn't quit loving each other. He was taken from me."

Marriage is compromise, though, so I took the pictures down and put them in the boys' room. When we would watch old home videos with Johnny in them, Keith would leave the room. I could tell he was uneasy any time we talked about Johnny. One day, I finally told him, "Johnny's name will never be a bad word in this house. Ever!"

He explained that he just thought the boys and I wanted those moments to ourselves. He didn't understand that I wanted him to share with us. But sometimes I think he felt he was in competition with Johnny. Not because of anything he did, but because I made him feel that way. I never intended to make him feel that way and it took me a long time to figure out how to quit doing it. On the flip side, Keith reminded the boys to be careful with Johnny's things, telling them to take care of them and put them back where they belonged. I can't figure it out for sure, but I think part of the jealousy comes from me never talking badly about Johnny. I choose to remember only the good. Those bad things mean nothing to me now. Johnny and I spent too much time arguing about silly things. We spent time when we refused to talk to each other and now I see that that time was wasted, taken from our time together.

With Keith, I decided that would not happen. We'd argue, and I'd just walk away to get myself together. I wanted to say what I needed to say and have the argument be over, and move on. Keith had a hard time adjusting to that and wanted to argue to prove his point. Most of the time he would raise his voice to drown me out and he would never hear what I had to say. It was easy to get mad at each other and not talk for days. Finally, I just said, "I'm not doing that!" I had learned the hard way. But then again, sometimes I forget that lesson and won't talk to him. Too many times we get comfortable with the people around us and we allow those previous lessons to fade away.

I felt like I had made it through the worst thing I could have imagined happening in my entire life, and then I found a wonderful man to marry. I was looking forward to a life with someone who was a friend first, someone God blessed me with. And it was still hard. I carried baggage into my marriage, and that is not good for a happy marriage. I could not put Keith before my boys. I know that is not good for a marriage, either. I just could not do it.

Keith was good for us, though, for me and for the boys. Keith could not replace Johnny, but he did step into the father role for them. Tyler didn't play baseball after Johnny died. He didn't want to do it because Johnny had always been his coach. After we got married, Tyler played again and Keith was his coach. Keith parents differently than Johnny did, too. The boys say Johnny was more serious whereas Keith is more playful. If something was broken, Johnny obsessed over what happened and how it happened. It bothered him. Keith can let things go much more easily. He has been good about letting the boys make their own decisions—and their own mistakes.

Even though he has been a father figure for the boys—he is a wonderful stepdad—he is not their father. They had their moments of arguments and disagreements that teenagers do. I know at least once one of the boys said "You're not my dad!" when they had a disagreement. I think all kids do that with a step-parent. I have protected Johnny as their dad. My dad was their primary father figure and then Keith moved into that role, but they don't call him "daddy." I heard Tyler once call Keith "Big Daddy," and I flew off the handle. "He is not your daddy! You will call him Keith!" I exclaimed. My mom tried to convince me to let Tyler call Keith whatever he wanted. She thought it was filling a need for Tyler, but I would not let it happen. I could not let it happen.

Keith hasn't only had to learn to live with the ghost of my dead husband. Johnny's killers also haunt us, in my dreams. About a year after we were married, three years after Johnny was killed, I dreamt that Otis and the others broke into our house. They were after my boys. I was crying in my sleep, and Keith woke me up. I vividly remember the dream and told Keith about it, fully awake. Although I realized it was a dream, I still felt the need to go and check on the boys, to ease my mind. The house was dark, and I didn't turn on any lights. I can hardly see anything anyway without my glasses, but, after checking on the boys, I walked back to my bedroom. Keith had bent over to pick something up from the floor, and I didn't see him. I ran right into him. I thought the killers were in our house. I screamed and cried. I thought my nightmare was real, even when I was awake.

With all my carrying on I woke Tyler and Jeffrey, but I did not tell them about the dream. I didn't want to scare them, too.

CHAPTER 23

THE HEAT

FROM THE DAY Johnny died, I worried constantly about not finding out who did it, or what would happen if they got off, if they were found not guilty. I worried about how Jeffrey and Tyler would feel if that happened. And I knew that I would give up all my worldly possessions if the people who killed Johnny would be punished for what they had done.

After meeting with the prosecutor and discussing the options of going to trial with all three men or trying each one individually, it was determined that separate trials would be the best course to take. I was a little hesitant and probably more anxious than anything to get them all at one time. I knew I had to do a crash course on the legal system to be certain that we were doing the right thing for Johnny. While I trusted the prosecutor without a doubt, at the same time I didn't like it when his office made decisions and I didn't have a clue why they were made, not that the solicitor would have done anything differently if I had asked. After all, it was the State of South Carolina vs. Otis, Shane and Robert, not Sheila Hanna-Wiles vs. Otis, Shane and Robert. I couldn't understand or comprehend how they were going to prosecute one at a time, and get convictions, until the prosecutor explained the reasoning of "The hand of one is the hand of all." According to this theory, "One who joins with another to accomplish an illegal purpose is liable criminally for everything done by his confederate incidental to the execution of the common design and purpose." [State v. Curry, 370 S.C. 674,684 (S.C. Ct. App. 2006)] The Supreme Court in South Carolina further expanded this in State v. Kelsey, 331 S.C. 50, 76-77, 502 S.E.2d 63, 76 (1998), in which it was held that "if a crime is committed by two or more persons who are acting together in the commission of a crime, then the act of one is the act of both."

I was convinced this was the best strategy and in our best interest. It was determined that Otis would be the first one to stand trial.

The trial was a roller-coaster of emotion. Anticipating justice was a high point for me. I knew that, no matter what the verdict, it would not bring Johnny back to us, but somehow I felt like a conviction would make us feel better, make our agony less intense. At least, I expected that it would be vindicating for us and, if nothing else, it would get one killer off the streets and help my family sleep better, knowing that at least one bad guy was put away. For us, and especially for my children, all that mattered was that they put away the most significant bad guy—the one who took their daddy away.

But there were also lows in the trial. Lots of them. It was so hard to hear, in horrifying detail, what happened to Johnny. The pathologist reported explicitly about each stab wound and what it did to Johnny's body. He explained each bullet's path and the damage it did. The attorneys asked questions like, "Could Johnny still talk after having his tongue slashed?" and there was detailed testimony about his body's reaction to the shot to his heart, and how he vomited on himself. My stomach churned and I felt a twinge in my body, like an echo of Johnny's pain convulsing through me. I tried to close my mind and my ears, but I still heard the horrible details about what Johnny endured before he finally died.

With this testimony, I realized that my pain and the boys' pain would not end as quickly as Johnny's life had ended. When you love someone, especially your children, you hurt when they hurt. Seeing your children in pain and being helpless to stop it is one of the most hopeless feelings.

For most of the trial, Tyler stayed with Mot and Stuart but sometimes, when I had to have him with me, he sat in the back of the courtroom with a victims-rights advocate, who kept him occupied with games and GI Joe men. Other times, I had him with me and my parents.

As a 911 telecommunicator, I heard frantic phone calls daily. I would do what I could to get the callers the help they needed, and then, sometimes, I wondered what became of them. But in the courtroom, it was my own young son who sat on the witness stand and listened to his own 911 phone call. While I looked on and listened with everyone else in court, I watched Jeffrey as his terrified little voice emanated from the machine, crying for help. It broke my heart. Tall and lean, Jeffrey looked sixteen but he was only twelve years old.

Like a horror movie, the scene played out. My little son, a frightened child, cried desperately for help, in fear for his life, terrorized by the brutal murderers who had killed his daddy, his protector, his hero. It did not seem real, hearing his sobs played back, and I felt sick as Christi asked him to go back into the laundry room to see if Johnny was still breathing. I was her supervisor and I knew well that she did the right thing, but I also knew what Jeffrey had seen, and how that momentary image had imprinted itself on Jeffrey's mind. He sounded so helpless, so scared. Christi dispatched the rescue squad and the police, which was all she could do, because Jeffrey knew that his daddy was dead. And he didn't know what monster might still be in that house with him and Tyler.

As the tape played my twelve-year-old son sat on the stand, listening to his own voice. He later said that it was like listening to someone else talking, and, being the protector, the strong one, he felt sorry for "that kid." Hearing his voice, he sobbed on the stand. Though he was only two years older than the version of himself on that recording, the adolescent heard the voice of the young boy with the strong southern accent and later said that he thought he sounded so naïve, so vulnerable—"ignorant." It was as if he heard some little kid talking, some stranger, saying those things. Oh, man, that's somebody super young, Jeffrey thought. He shouldn't be going through that. He knew that it was his own voice, his own experience, but at the same time he was overwhelmed by feeling sad that "somebody that young" was going through it. And, then, as he had flashes that it was himself, it felt even worse, hearing that helplessness and realizing that it was his own. "That was me," he realized. "That was me, with that helplessness in my voice. I was so helpless."

Jeffrey also had to testify to what he saw. A diligent and disciplined young man, he recalled every detail about how he recognized immediately that his father was dead, and how he feared that he and Tyler would be similarly killed at any moment. He told about how he got Tyler to hide with him in the corner, and how he wanted to get his back up against a wall so that he could see if anyone was coming after them.

At one point in the trial, Otis testified. I was holding Jeffrey in my lap, and Tyler was in my father's lap. Something Otis said upset Jeffrey, and he started crying. Tyler saw his big brother crying and started in, too. I held it together on the outside, but emotionally, I was at the bottom of that roller coaster with the weight of my whole family bearing down on me.

That emotional ride had some twists, too. Otis claimed that Paul and the investigating officers had set up a conspiracy to frame him for the murder, feeding him some of the details of the crime that he had talked about in his burglary plea bargain. He said that Paul told him what to say and that the officers showed him pictures and described the scene to him in detail, and that's how he knew. He claimed they told him that if he said he was at the scene but stayed the whole time in the truck, or car—even what kind of vehicle the killers drove that day became open to debate during the trial— that they would cut him a deal on the burglary conviction he was already serving and that way he could get out early. He wanted to get out of prison before his new wife got out.

At one point, he said that Shane Rice had told him all the details about the murder. Otis claimed that he himself wasn't even there that day and that Rice was the shooter. He said that he ran into Rice and hung out with him a bit and that's when Rice bragged about the murder and gave him the details. He also made those comments about Johnny and me fighting, and about some woman named Julia being at our house the night before the murder, while I was at work; since I was working the day shift, this was obvious a lie.

Otis's lies struck me as ironic. Knowing what a stand-up guy Johnny was and how he prided himself on teaching his boys to be honest, hardworking men, it was astonishing that someone could lie so many different ways. I wonder by his own admission in court about smoking crack, if it really messed with his understanding of right and wrong. Obviously, the only thing that Otis cared about was avoiding punishment, but it seemed like he told so many lies, he couldn't keep track of which story he was going with. At one point, he said he heard everything that he confessed from Shane Rice, but, at another point, he said it was all stuff he learned from Paul and the officers.

In that courtroom, we sat through it all while Otis's mom and sister tried to convince the jury that Otis was not at my house when this happened by saying he was mowing their grass all day on the day of the murder. They said they were there for hours while the kids went swimming and Otis cut the grass, never leaving the house. One of Otis's sisters testified that her son had band camp that morning, and she picked him up and took him to swim at her mom's house and saw Otis there. But, then, the prosecution called another witness—the band director, who testified that there was no band camp that Friday. I guess Otis's sister might have just confused the days.

The crazy ride of the trial had tricky turns, too. Otis's lawyers argued that his plea bargain, which he made in exchange for a lighter sentence on the burglaries, also applied to the murder charge. They argued before the trial even started that the plea agreement gave Otis immunity for the murder. Otis had made that agreement with the original prosecutor, Townes Jones, who ended up having to testify about the deal for the defense, and then another prosecutor had to handle the case. In the end, the judge agreed with the prosecution and determined that the plea covered the burglary, not the murder.

I don't know if we'll ever know whether Otis stabbed Johnny with a knife or shot him with a gun—or sat in the getaway car. I have my feelings about it and my boys and our other family members have their own theories, too. Since Otis knew Johnny, and Johnny could have identified Otis, he had the greatest motive for murder—to avoid leaving a witness—so that's one thing that makes me think that it might have been Otis. On the other hand, somebody dropped that bag out in the cornfield, and Otis seemed to be the only one who knew about it. That made me think that, when Otis saw Johnny, he took off running while the other guys fought with Johnny, which would mean that Otis wasn't the one that actually did the killing. The police didn't agree with that theory. They said that they thought he was the killer and that he knew about that bag because one of the other guys told him. That could be true. I don't know. We may never know who did what.

Legally, it doesn't matter. The prosecuting attorney on the case, Knox McMahon, said in his closing arguments something that I've tried to teach my kids: "The hand of one is the hand of all." Being a part of doing wrong is doing wrong. Standing by while despicable things are done to another human being is despicable. McMahon argued that, even if Otis stayed in the getaway vehicle, as he confessed, he was still guilty of murder because he was a part of the murder that the group committed. The jury agreed. On November 23, 2002, the jury convicted Otis of Johnny's murder.

Right before the judge was going to hand down the sentence we, the family, were allowed to speak to the court and give our thoughts on sentencing. Marshall and Lynn both spoke about how much they missed their son and brother and asked the judge to give Otis the hardest sentence he could. And then it was my turn to speak on behalf of Johnny, the boys, and myself. I had a lot to say, and wrote down everything I wanted the judge to hear. I said:

On August 6, 1999, my family was torn apart. I lost my husband and my best friend. My children lost their daddy and their role model. On that day, in a matter of minutes, me and my children became homeless. Johnny was the strength behind our family. He loved our boys more than anything and even though he is not here to speak for himself I know the heartache he would have felt knowing our sons' had been traumatized by Otis's actions on August 6, 1999. Johnny coached both of our children in baseball and enjoyed every part of being a father. He was looking forward to the different aspects of life raising two sons. But he never got the chance to enjoy them. He didn't get to be there when Jeffrey hit his first home run or when he hit his first baseball over the fence to win the ballgame. He didn't get to see Tyler when he rode his four-wheeler for the first time by himself. Nor did he get to take Tyler on his first camping trip with the Cub Scouts and he didn't get to see him get baptized. And he won't get to see them drive a car, date, graduate, or be their best man at their wedding. And he won't have the opportunity to enjoy our grandchildren that he and I would talk and laugh about. On August 6, 1999, our children were only six and ten years old and they were confronted with something most adults couldn't handle and that day will forever be implanted in their memory of their daddy.

The effects this has had on Jeffrey and Tyler…Tyler didn't want to play baseball because his daddy was not there to coach him. Tyler experienced nightmares and still to this day. Jeffrey lost his childhood completely. Johnny used to tell Jeffrey when he would leave to go to work, "I'm not going to be here so you're the man of the house. Take care of Mama and Tyler." Jeffrey followed his daddy's instructions and has tried very hard to fill the shoes of an adult. Every bit of innocence that my children had before Johnny's death was taken away. The impact of Johnny's death for me was emotional and financial. Johnny was the main provider for our family. We were very proud of our hard work and what we had accomplished in such a short time. We were buying our house and eleven acres of land. We both drove two nice vehicles. I couldn't make the payments on my salary alone and I was faced with trying to find a home for me and my boys. With the help of family and friends and most importantly God's guidance, I was eventually able to purchase another home. Strong-willed and determined, I made changes to help me keep the land and house that Johnny and I purchased together, although I hate to this day to go back to that house. I would like to mention some of the articles that Otis stole from our home and the effects it had:

- Johnny's wedding band—I won't be able to pass this down to Jeffrey or Tyler
- My wedding rings—Sentimental value
- Home videos—He stole all the videos of Johnny coaching the boys in baseball from 1996 to 1999. Our Christmas during those years. Each and everything we did during that time period.
- A watch from his father—Would have been an heirloom.

The other things that were taken were of value but do not have the sentimental value attached to them. Regardless, all those items were ours and not Otis's or anybody else's. To try and put the emotional effect of the past three years on paper would be impossible. I loved Johnny more than anything. I was a part of him and he was a part of me. That day when Otis assisted in killing Johnny he took a part of me too. I will forever have an empty place in my heart. Furthermore, Johnny's murder was indirectly responsible for the death of his mother. The same month two years later, Barbara, Johnny's mother committed suicide. Johnny got saved and baptized along with me and Jeffrey three weeks before his death so I know that Johnny is in a better place but he didn't deserve the way he got there. In conclusion, no matter what type sentence you give to Otis it will not bring Johnny back. But if we, Johnny's family, are sentenced to a life of heartache and grief I believe the person responsible for that should be sentenced to life also. We won't ever have a chance at parole and neither should Otis. Your Honor, I hope and pray that you consider our suffering, feelings and suggestion when you hand down Otis's sentence.

Thank you and God Bless You, Sheila, Jeffrey and Tyler Hanna

Sentenced to life in prison, Otis refused to testify against Rice or Robert, so the police struggled to make a case against either of them. Otis continued to argue that his plea bargain should have protected him from the murder conviction, and he appealed, but his conviction was affirmed.

CHAPTER 24
THERE IS NO SUCH THING AS CLOSURE

IN 1999, THE year when Johnny died, 282 other people were murdered in South Carolina. My husband was the only murder victim I have ever known, and yet I believe that the loved ones of all of those other victims experienced many of the same emotions that my family and I did. That means that, in South Carolina alone and in 1999 as a whole, probably thousands of people—wives and husbands, mothers and fathers, sons and daughters, and brothers and sisters of the other 282 murder victims—suffered the nightmares, horror, rage, and agony that we endured.

I imagine that nearly all of those survivors of murder believed, as I did, that we would celebrate—or at least feel better—when the murderer of our loved one was arrested, convicted, and sentenced. But we all learned the hard way that the proclamation of the word "Guilty" and the declaration of a sufficient sentence would do little to alleviate our pain. The myth of "closure" creates nothing more than cruel yearning and devastating disappointment. There is no such thing as closure.

But that does not mean that justice is irrelevant, Justice is very important to our healing. When the detectives investigate, states prosecute, jurors convict, and judges pass sentence, they affirm that our murdered loved one matters. Though the police, prosecutors, jury, and judge never knew Johnny, their passion for their work and their diligence in doing it sent my family and me a strong message: The hole in my heart matters. My sons' horrific experience matters. Their deprivation of their father matters. And it matters that the world is deprived of Johnny Hanna.

This is how justice helps. It provides a certain sense of satisfaction and validation of the value of our loss. Still, it feels inadequate, for how can anyone possibly understand the depth of this pain, especially when they did not know what an incredible man we lost? In that sense, I think, we survivors tend to feel that the justice system came up short. Otis got life without the possibility of parole. Objectively, I guess, that is an appropriate sentence but, emotionally, it hurts deeply knowing for the rest of my life I will fight to keep Otis in prison. I will respond and be present at every appeal. This is not closure. Do I wish he had received the death penalty? No. I think that death would have been too easy on him. I want Otis to suffer with guilt, to live many years, yearning every day for freedom and regretting that he took Johnny from us. I want Otis to realize that Johnny's life matters.

On the other hand, the lack of justice is an extremely difficult obstacle to our healing. Without justice, we feel as if the value of our loss—the value of Johnny's life—is diminished, as if society has determined that the freedom of a couple of violent crack heads is more important than the life of a gregarious, fun, hardworking, disciplined, and good man. Of course, "society" has not made such a determination, but that is how it feels, and I continue—always—to yearn for justice for the other suspects in Johnny's murder. When Otis was convicted and sentenced, my sons and I were left with a daunting and palpable fear that justice will never be satisfied, since the authorities had insufficient evidence to try the other defendants, Shane Rice and Robert Compton. It seemed that the only chance we had to prosecute them rested with Otis as a witness, and he had learned well to keep his mouth shut—though too late to keep himself free of responsibility. Despite Otis's fate, we suffer in knowing that the other likely perpetrators got away with murder. And it is not just the knowing. We also carry anger and fantasies of revenge, some of us more than others.

As soon as the jury came back with its verdict, I was overjoyed. I think I even cried a little bit, but it was temporary. It only lasted for a few minutes. At some point, I realized that the fight for justice had been just another avenue of how to cope; a distraction, in a way. And, once it was over, life was still just as sad as it had been.

Hindsight is 20/20 but, looking back, I realize that the boys started to suppress their memories in those first few years and, especially for Tyler, that was a big part of the tragedy. I still hadn't realized that Tyler had seen Johnny dead, so I didn't understand that he, like Jeffrey, would try to forget those images. Since Jeffrey was ten when Johnny died, he could remember much of his life with Johnny even though part of his brain worked to forget the horror. But Tyler was too young.

Over the years, I didn't know that Tyler's main thought of his daddy—his number-one memory—was the image of Johnny, dead. Tyler thought about that more than thinking of the earlier memories, more than the happy times, more than the family life that he'd had with his father. At the top of his mind when Johnny's name came up, was death, not life. So Tyler, at seven, eight, and nine years old, had begun to try to forget the horror because it was about all he remembered, and as he tried to forget his traumatic memories, he lost most of his good memories, too. It was a terribly high price for him to pay because, in the end, he lost almost all of them.

Meanwhile, I was focused on Jeffrey because I knew what he had seen and I knew that it had to be harmful for a child his age to have to deal with such a traumatic image, not to mention his tremendous fear. By the time the trial was over, the fear was not as daunting, but I knew that it was still with Jeffrey. It would always be.

Jeffrey got into some fights. Often, he had reasons. Before and after Johnny died, Jeffrey would fight because he was taking up for himself or for other people who couldn't or wouldn't defend themselves. But sometimes, after Johnny died, I think that he knew that he wouldn't get into as much trouble with me as he might have with Johnny. At least, if I had to spank him, it wouldn't hurt as bad as when Johnny used to do it.

Jeffrey and Tyler used to fight a lot, too. With four years between them, they had a lot of sibling rivalry at this time and acted as if they despised each other. They fought all the time and it was hard for me. One time, Tyler recalls, he and Jeffrey got into a fight about Tyler not crying for his daddy. Of course, Jeffrey never cried in front of me, but apparently it bothered him that Tyler didn't, either, and Tyler only remembers that he didn't because it was cause for a dispute between them. It's possible that Jeffrey saw it as his job to supervise such issues where his younger brother was concerned.

That year, the spring after the trial, both of the boys played baseball and Keith helped as Tyler's coach. It was like a normal life and, despite everything; I started to feel so blessed. I realized that God had given me so much, with such fine and talented sons, and I was proud of both of them. I was also blessed with a wonderful husband who was a great stepdad to my sons and I realized that, after all the bad things that had happened to us, we really were blessed with a good life.

At eight years old, Tyler played baseball with the recreation department and, by then, it was obvious that he was the spitting imagine of his daddy. He acted like Johnny, too. Stocky and built on a hefty frame, Tyler was athletic like Johnny, more like a football player than a baseball player, and he reminded me so much of his daddy. It was a comfort to look at Tyler that way, like a miniature Johnny.

Though Jeffrey had Johnny's height he was lean, not stocky. He was also well-mannered and shared Johnny's temperament, but Jeffrey was definitely more of a baseball player. By that spring, he played a lot of baseball. During the week he would play with other kids, looking pretty mature for a thirteen-year-old as he pitched or played in the infield. On the weekends, he also played softball in an adult league. Jeffrey played third base on a team full of twenty- and thirty-year-old men, even one forty-year-old guy. The guys had to be eighteen to play so, when the team went to play in tournaments, Jeffrey would have to lie about his age. When asked, he told the tournament officials that he'd had a DUI and his license had been taken away.

Jeffrey's high school started when he was thirteen, in eighth grade. That's where he met Tosha, when they had Geography class together. They became friends and dated for a short period of time in eighth grade.

Though I felt like my life had gotten better, with great sons, a wonderful new husband that I loved, and a normal family life, I still thought about Johnny every single day. I still wondered what my life would have been like if he had been there. I thought about what we would have been doing. And, I realized, I would never know. I also felt like maybe I should have gotten over what happened, and knew well that I hadn't yet. I wondered if I ever would.

CHAPTER 25

SHAME AND PRIDE

I N AN IRONIC TWIST, Tyler knew Otis's daughter, Joy, from riding the school bus together. They were the last houses on the route so they rode together for a long ride every day, coming and going, and by the fifth and sixth grades, when Jeffrey was in high school, Tyler and Joy talked on the bus. He tried not to talk to her whenever Jeffrey was around, and to have nothing to do with her, because he knew that Jeffrey wouldn't tolerate her. So it wasn't exactly a friendship, but they were acquainted. They never talked about the murder. Once, though, they talked about something to do with the trial or Otis. Tyler doesn't remember what she said, but he said, "If I tell my mama, will you tell her what you told me?" She said yes, and wrote something down on a piece of paper, which she gave to Tyler. He remembers giving it to me. Of course, as soon as I read it I called the Chief and he came out and picked it up. It said that she had overheard her mama and Angel talking and that Angel was there, too, on the day of the murder. Chief Johnson went out and talked to Joy about it, and she recounted it all.

I ran into Joy myself, in the fall of 2004. She had been coming every now and then to the youth meetings at church, but I had not run into her until one night, when I was going to give my testimony to the Youth Group. As

I was preparing for my testimony, one of the youth leaders came and told me that Joy was in attendance. I said that I needed to talk to Joy before I started so Joy, the youth leader, and I all went outside. I explained to her that I was giving my testimony and it involved what happened to Johnny. I promised not to bring up her father's name and said that I wouldn't bring any embarrassment to her. She got angry and called me a liar. "If they want to stay and listen to your lies, then that is their choice," she shouted. "But I'm not staying!" She left.

I was shaken, but I got through the night. The thing is that I was aware that lots of different people—including Joy—had different views about us. In fact, after Johnny died, I thought a lot about how people on "the outside" saw us. I knew that most people thought of us as "that poor family," and of Jeffrey and Tyler as "those poor boys." In some ways, they were right. We suffered the greatest sadness, the greatest loss. Our lives were turned upside down and completely changed, but all of that is not the worst thing. The worst thing is that those murderers took my sons' memories from them. They were robbed of the memories they had, and the memories that they could have made with their daddy.

The thing that hurt the most, especially as the years ticked by, was that the boys could not remember Johnny. Tyler was so young—and so traumatized—when Johnny died, so he doesn't remember, and that hurts. I know that Johnny loved the boys more than his own life. In his eyes, the sun would rise and set on the boys. Tyler, especially, can't remember or enjoy that. That has always made me so angry for what they lost.

The other big thing that the killers took from Jeffrey and Tyler was the most important person who could have impacted their lives. So many times after it happened, I thought, *Oh, God, why couldn't it have been me?* Boys don't need their mama like they need their father. So, one minute I was angry and then the next minute I was sad, thinking that, if my sons had their choice of which parent they could have, at that age they would have wanted their daddy. How do you replace the father? I knew that I couldn't and I felt so inadequate being the mother of two fatherless boys. It made me ever more grateful that we had Keith in our lives, but also made me so much more angry that my kids had been robbed of their father and of their childhood memories.

It wasn't just anger and sadness. I worried, especially about Tyler. I knew that Jeffrey was old enough—had enough years with his father—so that he was deeply influenced by Johnny. Still, I imagine what he didn't get because he was only ten. He was just growing out of that age of needing his mother, just becoming old enough that male role models were everything. As he grew up, I could see that he really had Johnny's values. But Tyler was so young that he hadn't really learned those lessons yet. He was too young to learn those things, or even to get a sense of them. Still, Tyler had so much of Johnny in him. He liked the outdoors, just like his daddy did, and constantly reminded me of him.

Sometimes, if he did something wrong and I had to discipline or scold him, he would answer back to me, "If Daddy was here, he would let me do it." He'd give it to me. I thought that, deep down, he actually felt that way, but I also figured that he felt that, if he threw his dad into it, I would give in, because I gave in to everything when it came to their dad. But it was still so hard, and it was a fine line that was hard to cross. Especially with Tyler, I wanted to give him as much of his dad as I could, and I wanted to instill those values that Johnny gave Jeffrey, and hope that Jeffrey gave them to Tyler. So, when Tyler would try to say that Johnny would have given in, I would disagree. "No, your dad wouldn't," I said. "Your dad would have agreed with me because of this, this, and this…" Tyler would continue to argue the point until Jeffrey jumped in. "Daddy would have agreed with Mama," Jeffrey would say. Then Tyler believed it.

This gave them a unique relationship and a special connection. Tyler knows that Jeffrey had experience with Johnny and memories of him that Tyler missed out on so, in a way, Tyler depends on Jeffrey to share his knowledge. Tyler pulls for Jeffrey to share his memories, even his memories of the murder scene.

Since Tyler had trouble remembering Johnny as a father, he always wanted to learn all he could about Johnny and the kind of man that he was. That included learning about his daddy's life before he became a good, solid family man.

Some people remember Johnny being a strong man and, when he was younger, a fighter. Hungry for information about his father, Tyler learned about some of those stories about Johnny, and then he wanted to have that same reputation. People would tell Tyler stories about Johnny but, since Tyler was at a rebellious age in his own life, he picked up on some of the more colorful stories from those times in Johnny's life that Tyler thought were more exciting than the man Johnny became as his father. As a result, Tyler has struggled some, wanting to be known as a tough guy. While he is not a troublemaker and he doesn't go around starting fights, he has been in a handful of fights and, at times, has glorified that aspect of his father's youth.

More than anything else that he has lost, Tyler lacked memories of his father, so he started listening intently whenever people told stories about the legacy and reputation of Johnny Hanna, the gregarious man with hundreds of friends and the strong football player whom no one could roll over. From a fairly young age, that's the side of Johnny that Tyler wanted to emulate.

His whole life, whether Tyler heard stories about his daddy or saw his cousins living large, all he wanted in life was to be like Hanna men, like his daddy, and he always sought to learn what that meant. As a teenager, he latched on to some of the more rebellious behaviors that he saw or heard about, and wanted to follow them more than anything.

Tyler took Johnny's reputation as a Hanna—and his own—seriously. If he saw Hanna cousins fighting, Tyler wanted to fight. If he saw them with lots of girlfriends, he wanted to be a ladies man. Tyler wanted to be a Hanna. He had to be a Hanna.

He got into a few fights at school because, if anyone started something with Tyler, "he would finish it." If he didn't, he figured that Jeffrey would finish it later, so Tyler always saw to it that he won. In the seventh grade, a big kid, at least six-foot-two, often picked on Tyler who acted just like Johnny in not backing away. Tyler picked on the other kid right back, and they ended up getting into some scrapes. Though Tyler wasn't as tall as the other boy he was broad and strong and relentless, so he won.

Until high school, Tyler was rebellious. He didn't want to do what people told him to do and, often, it was Keith doing the telling. Tyler would sleep in the living room and leave his stuff lying around the room and on the floor, and Keith would tell him to pick it up. Tyler was stubborn and refused. By the time Keith was ready to go to work, he'd had enough. "Do it now," he'd say. "Before I leave." Tyler fussed at Keith, who just walked off to his room to get ready for work. Tyler did what he had to do, but grudgingly. Whenever Tyler pushed and it was a problem for me or Keith, Jeffrey handled it. Jeffrey would get the response from Tyler that Keith and I couldn't get.

In our area, high school starts in the eighth grade. When Tyler was about to start high school at Jeffrey's school, the boys talked about what Tyler could expect. Jeffrey warned Tyler that the upper classmen would probably try to push him around. He told Tyler that he would have to defend himself. Since Tyler was bigger and stronger than most kids his age, he wanted to set boundaries as soon as he started high school, so that the older kids would realize that he was not a new kid that they could push around. Tyler got into a few fights that year until he established his reputation as a strong guy who stood up for himself. By the ninth grade, though, he grew out of it and made friends with everybody. Then he changed completely. Jeffrey had him lifting weights and Tyler started playing football, and he grew up.

Still, sometimes my boys acted like they hated each other. They fought with each other all through high school. If Jeffrey brought home a girl, Tyler would bother him and want to hang around with them, and then Jeffrey would give him some brotherly taps, as Jeffrey calls it. In the mornings, when they were getting ready for school, Jeffrey wanted to sleep as long as he could so he wanted Tyler to get up earlier, take his shower, and get out of the bathroom before Jeffrey needed to get in there. If Tyler was slow about accomplishing his morning routine to clear the way for his brother, Jeffrey would pounce on him. Tyler credits his brother for making him a better fighter and a better man who, like his father, won't take heat from anyone.

Jeffrey got into a little bit of trouble—a few fights—but that was about it. Throughout high school he never even smoked a cigarette. Lots of people around our area smoke, including myself, but Jeffrey can't stand it so he never wanted to try cigarettes. He never smoked marijuana, either, though most of his friends have at least tried it. Often, he was the only person in a group who didn't smoke pot. He was never the kind of guy who would give in to peer pressure, and everybody who knew him was aware of that, so if someone offered him something and he said no, that would be the end of it. If it wasn't, if they pressed him, his anger would jump and he'd say, "Look, I told you no, okay?"

Partly I know that he didn't want to cause me any pain, so he was especially compliant. But he was also very conscientious and responsible and did not want to get into trouble with the police or anyone else. Jeffrey was always determined to succeed in life, and getting arrested for pot or the like would be counterproductive. Even at a young age, he knew that. Besides, he really didn't care to do drugs because he knew that it wasn't right. I like to think that some of his reasoning would be that I preached to both boys that drugs were the core cause of what happened to Johnny and, if they chose to go down that road, then they were no better than the people who killed their daddy. I realize that is a harsh thing to say to two young boys, but at the time it was the only way I could think of that would make the impression I wanted. I said this often enough that I'm confident that it got through to both of them.

Jeffrey says that, down in the Calhoun Falls area, pot is the most popular recreational drug. Up in Iva, meth is the drug of choice. But at Jeffrey and Tyler's school drinking was the most common, and Jeffrey wasn't immune to it. Most of the kids around there drank whatever they could get ahold of, and Jeffrey joined in with this partying. He never got in trouble with it, though. Sometimes, if the police caught a bunch of kids drinking, they would just deliver them to their parents, though Jeffrey never got hauled home. He never got into much trouble.

As I taught him, Jeffrey believed that if a person did hard drugs, they wouldn't be able to afford their habit and the drugs would cause them to become a thief, which is in the same category as a rapist and a murderer. "Listen," he told his friends, "If you smoke weed, that's your choice, but if you start bringing these people around that are doing the harder stuff we are going to have problems." He just could not be around people doing hard drugs, like meth. "One of us would have to leave," he said. "I couldn't be around that, because he's going to be the one breaking into people's houses, stealing, and killing people."

And killing people's dads.

During this time, Keith and I bought a restaurant in Iva called the Waffle King, which we renamed the Iva Buffet and Grill. It was an experience and not an altogether good one, though there were some good things. The boys both worked there during their high school years, which was good for them. They learned a lot about how to treat people and earning their own money. But Keith didn't like the hassles of owning a restaurant and he fell into a depression because of it. I hoped to make it work for us, but it wasn't long before we started talking about selling it.

The restaurant was only one part of the problem. Keith and I had lost some of the strength of our relationship, and I kept hoping we could recover what we used to have. I realized that, in the first years of our marriage, I never doubted that he loved me but I had started to doubt in his continued devotion, and I had no idea when it had started to fall apart. I hoped and prayed, often, that we would get it back.

Thinking about our relationship and working at it, I started to question myself a lot, and then I noticed things that I did that I couldn't get over. I saw that I was having trouble moving forward, so I knew that I was the majority of our problem. That's not to say that Keith is completely innocent, by no means. But I knew that I still had issues that I had to deal with. It was a hard time.

To make it even harder, my dad's health was not good and he was diagnosed with congestive heart failure. The doctor put him on oxygen, 24/7, for the rest of his life. I tried to talk to Dad about accepting Jesus but he would not listen, so I prayed that he would get right with the Lord before it was too late.

All of this was so hard on my mama. She had to run the store and she had another job, too. I desperately wished that I could have helped her, like paying off all of her bills, so she didn't have to work so hard while Dad was so sick. But, despite all of it, she held up well.

Through it all, the boys were a positive force in my life. I was so proud of them and watching them grow up and watching their activities gave me things to look forward to. In eleventh grade Jeffrey was a great ballplayer, a pitcher and third baseman who won All-Region and All-State honors. He had dreams of playing ball, but in tenth grade Jeffrey's vision started to get bad. It got worse and worse until he couldn't read the scoreboard by his senior year, so it was pretty hard to play baseball. He tried to wear glasses, but said that they affected his depth perception. During the medical screening for the Air Force, he failed the depth perception test which disqualified him for certain jobs. Then he had a shoulder injury, tearing up the labrum and other cartilage in his throwing arm. He was a pitcher, so it was a devastating injury. After shoulder surgery he returned to play third base, not his best position. As soon as he started throwing, his shoulder would hurt and he had to throw a different way, not as hard as he used to. In the end, he became an average player and his dreams of playing baseball were destroyed.

Through high school Jeffrey and Tosha became closer friends, though he had other girlfriends during high school, including one girl from ninth to eleventh grade. But then, when Jeffrey was sixteen, he started dating Tosha. Since they were already close friends, they were at ease with each other on dates, and they had a comfortable relationship. Jeffrey brought her to the house on Super Bowl Sunday in 2006, and they were a couple from that day forward.

In the beginning of the summer of 2006, I encountered Joy at church again. I was the leader for our young women's group, and we were beginning our "True Love Waits" study. Joy came. When she got to the church that Sunday evening, she was told that she could join her age group, which was meeting in my room.

As she entered the room, my heart sank. I asked her if she wanted to join our study, and I explained that it was a study about abstaining from sex until marriage. I added that, if she could make that commitment, then she would be a part of the ceremony that would be held later that year.

She agreed to participate in the study, which lasts eight weeks. I was really uncomfortable with Joy being in the class because I didn't know what to expect from her. A true extrovert, she was like a bomb waiting to explode and I was absolutely not going to let our history come to light in this class, with all the other girls there. So, during the first few meetings, I sort of tiptoed around her.

I don't really know what made the change—God, probably—but I was determined that I could help make a difference in her life and I was not going to let my fear of confrontation slow me down. And that is just what I did. If she said or did something that I thought was disrespectful or shouldn't be shared then I would let her know, and I was constantly talking to her about her grades in school and how important school was. One time, I asked her what her dream life would be and I was shocked when she said that she didn't know because she had never thought about it. I thought all kids had dreams.

On the second or third meeting, the class was wrapping up and I was saying good-bye to the girls when Joy came up to me and said she needed to talk to me. Since she had not fully opened herself up to me in the previous few weeks, I immediately feared that it was going to be some type of confrontation. I could tell she was uncomfortable around me and I was uneasy around her, too. Instead, she asked me a simple question: "How can I be saved?"

I was stunned. I shared the Plan of Salvation with her and led her in the Sinner's Prayer. She was excited. I was overjoyed for her and I let her know it, and I think I just went numb. I was truly confused. After she left, I sat by myself in my church room and cried. After a few minutes, I went to find our pastor and tell him what just happened. "How could God put me in that position?" I asked.

The weeks of the study went by. It was going well and, as the True Love Ceremony neared, I told the girls that I needed each of them to give me the name of the person who would place the ring on their finger. Joy came up to me and asked if I would place her ring during the ceremony. I told her I would be happy to, but I encouraged her to ask her mom.

Some of the girls did not have money to purchase a nice outfit for the ceremony so we held a fundraiser and raised enough money to help buy outfits for those who couldn't afford them, including Joy. We set a date to go dress shopping and out to eat. We headed out on our shopping spree on a Saturday morning and shopped all day. The girls were excited to go shopping and I was excited because it was the first time we had done anything like this at our church. It was a terrific day.

During the week before the ceremony, I heard rumors that Joy had been suspended from school. I planned to confront her about the rumors on the day of the ceremony, but she did not show up. I asked a few people if they had seen her, but they all said no. More than anything I was concerned for her, and I was disappointed because I thought that she was getting on the right track. I never saw her again.

A few days later, I sent a letter to Otis, in prison:

Dear Otis,

I hope this letter finds you doing as good as can be expected. You may not read this letter in its completion but my prayer is that you will. I know you are probably surprised to hear from me because I am surprised that I have come this far to be able to write to you. I want to share with you some things that have happened in the past few years. I prayed almost daily for God to give me the courage and show me the way to forgive you. I know that you still claim your innocence and you have that right but I also have the right to believe the evidence that was presented in the trial.

You may throw this letter away right now without reading any further but I hope you don't. The day that Johnny was killed changed my life and my boys' lives forever. We miss him every day. I started this letter with the intention of telling you everything that me and my boys have been through since Johnny's death but I don't think that is what God has placed on my heart to share with you at this time.

I thought for the past few years that I had forgiven you but I truly did not forgive you until the last few months and that is why I am sending you this letter. From the very beginning when you were arrested for Johnny's murder my main concern was your daughter, Joy. She was an innocent child that didn't deserve the cards that life had dealt her. For the past few years I would always ask anyone that I came into contact with, that knew Joy, how she was doing. Joy made a comment to one of my sons about wanting to come to Church. I made arrangements for a Church member to pick Joy up and bring her to Church. Joy is now a part of the Lowndesville Baptist Church Young Women's Group, which I am the leader.

A little over a month ago, Joy stayed after class and asked me what she needed to do to be Saved. After explaining what she needed to do, Joy asked Jesus Christ into her heart. I left Church that night ecstatic about Joy's decision but couldn't figure out why God used me to be the one to share His Salvation Plan with Joy. And then it just came to me that God was leading me through Joy to forgive you. Joy is very special to me and I want to see her succeed in everything that she does. I asked her one day after we had been shopping when was the last time that she went to see you. She stated that she had not seen you since the trial. I told her that the Church would be glad to bring her to see you, all she had to do was ask. She said that she needed to get her personal information in before she could come and see you. I pray that you will encourage her and guide her in her Christian walk. I know she is struggling about going to school so maybe if you let her know the importance of getting her education she will put forth the effort of bettering herself.

You might be thinking that you couldn't help her because you are in prison but you can help her. If you don't want her to travel down the road that you traveled then be honest with her about your past and let her know that you are concerned with the road she chooses to travel. Our children are precious and God demands that we lead them in the right way, regardless, if we are with them every day or if we must guide them behind prison walls.

The other reason for this letter is to let you know that I do forgive you. Sure there are questions that I would like answers to such as, Why? What did Johnny ever do to you to make you kill him? What exactly happened the day that Johnny was killed? Did he beg for his life? I hope and pray that you will dig deep in your heart to give me these answers one day. It won't bring Johnny back but it will allow me to bring about some type of closure.

In closing, I want to tell you that Joy needs your guidance and your support. She loves you (I know that because she told me) and wants to have a relationship with you. My boys won't have the opportunity to have a relationship with their father, but Joy does have that opportunity and it is up to you to make it happen.

It didn't take long before his mother called me and told me not to write to Otis again, adding that he was not guilty. I know Otis' family was hurting too, and I was upset when his mother called me. I didn't write the letter to hurt them or Otis. I just wanted the truth and was desperate, still, for everyone to be held responsible. I wanted him to help Joy and finally I wanted him to know that I had forgiven him.

CHAPTER 26

THE EASY WAY OUT

SHANE RICE SPENT a few years in jail, from October, 2000, to June, 2003. And then a few years later, on December 13, 2006, he hung himself in his backyard.

I had known his father, but I knew nothing else about Shane, except that he was arrested and charged with murdering Johnny. I heard that he left a note that said he couldn't live with what he had done, or something to that effect. It was vague, didn't specify any regrets about Johnny, and did not confess what he felt guilty for, a confession would have helped so much in our healing process. As far as we were concerned, he took the easy way out. His suicide left us angry. We wanted him to admit to what he had done— for him to take responsibility for it. We wanted him to spend his life in jail. His suicide was just another disappointment for us. Death is always hard on the family and I am sure this was hard for his family. So again our two families were hurting.

I felt like I was just going through the motions of everyday life, but I was never moving on. I was able to go for a couple of days without thinking about Johnny and his death, but then it would hit me again, and then I would feel terribly guilty for not thinking about him.

The biggest thing, the heavy feeling I carried with me all the time, was that I knew in my heart—without a doubt—that, if the situation was changed, if I was the one who had been killed that day, that Johnny would not rest until every single person was held accountable. Because I was so certain of that, I felt an obligation to do the same. I felt like I just couldn't rest until Shane Rice and Robert Compton were tried. And then Rice took away that possibility.

At the same time, for practical purposes, I had such a good life. Keith got a good job at Michelin, though he had to work really hard. I felt blessed to have him in my life, as well as his son, and my boys were doing well, too. When the boys were both in high school, it seemed like the time flew by. Thinking about Jeffrey leaving for college made me feel pangs of empty nest syndrome, though my nest was still full. Jeffrey and Tyler both played football, and they both had girlfriends. Jeffrey and Tosha were good together, and Tyler started dating as well. I was grateful for my life but, still, something was amiss. I wasn't "over it."

I prayed that God would help bring closure to me, my sons, Marshall, and Johnny's sister Lynn. Despite the letdown of Otis's conviction, and the fact that it felt like a partial victory, I still felt like my emotional healing rested in justice and vindication. I wanted more. And even though Shane was dead, I still wanted his guilt or innocence to be determined, once and for all.

At one point, the Sheriff turned over Johnny's case file to the South Carolina Law Enforcement Division, and I was hopeful that they would find something that had been overlooked. I kept hoping and praying that my phone would ring and, at the other end, the chief or the sheriff would tell me that they'd found it, the evidence they needed to hold the other two responsible. As time went by, I just hoped that they would make more arrests in my lifetime.

I wanted justice to help Jeffrey and Tyler to find a new way to cope with what had happened. If we could have brought the other responsible people to justice, that would have given my boys another way to cope and another vehicle to help them move on. Justice would have opened another door for them.

But my hopes for justice dwindled, and, in time, I just hoped that Jeffrey and Tyler would be able to live their lives and let the past remain in their past. I carried such hurt, disappointment, agony, and worry, and I didn't want that for them. *God, watch over Jeffrey and Tyler, I prayed. Keep them safe and out of harm's way. I hope I have raised them right with good morals. Allow them to enjoy life to the fullest and, when I'm not present, make sure they make the right choices and let them feel Your presence. I pray that they will always keep You first in their lives.*

As an adult, I felt so much emotion—anger, sadness—that controlled my life, and I didn't want that for them. I wanted them to be able to move on. But I also wanted to be the adult, someone they could depend on. I wanted to be the one to deal with all of it so that they could just be okay, without the feelings that I carried. I wanted to take the hurt, the anger, and the pain, to bear all of that so that they could have decent and normal lives. Since their childhood was marred by tragedy, I wanted them to be able to enter their adult lives without it. I wanted them to have the same chance at normalcy that anyone else had.

As a mother, I had to know a few things in my heart. One, I had to know that I gave them every opportunity, every outlet, to express how they felt so that they could move on. Two, I wanted them to see that, even though something so bad happened, that there is a dessert in it. And the dessert for each of us is different. For me, it was no longer closure, because I realized there really is no closure. I started to realize that, if we looked for closure, we would be closing out an important part of our lives, and I desperately hoped that my boys would never do that. For me, the dessert was that Johnny's life—and his death—had a testimony, which I wanted to share. My boys and I suffered things that people don't normally hear about, but we came out of it with our faith and God and each other, and I felt that this was something beautiful, something to share.

I also wanted Jeffrey and Tyler to be able to live a normal life every single day. I knew that it wouldn't be normal normal, but I wanted it to be normal for us. I wanted to be able to tell my grandbabies—someday—about their grandfather, Johnny Hanna. I wanted to share our family videos with them and show them what their daddies were like when they were children with Johnny. I wanted Jeffrey and Tyler to be able to talk about their father without crying because I wanted his memory to be a joyful thing.

In May, 2007, when Jeffrey graduated from high school, it was hard for me. His graduation was the first big event in our family since Johnny died and, while I was so happy for Jeffrey, I just couldn't get excited because Johnny wasn't there to share it. For me, it was the hardest day. Still, I knew that Jeffrey did not look at it the way I did. I know he would have given anything to have had Johnny there, but it wasn't the most important thing to him that day. For me, it was.

CHAPTER 27

A MAN OF DISCIPLINE

TYLER WAS SCARED of Jeffrey—really scared, from the brotherly point of view— and he would listen to Jeffrey a lot more than he did me. When Tyler was a younger teenager, he would really try my patience and push me to the limit. And I did everything I could think of—grounded him, spanked him. I did it all, and I was not getting through to him. At one point, Tyler pulled his arm back like it crossed his mind to hit me. I knew he would never have hit me, but he had pulled his arm back like that. I didn't know what to do so I found Jeffrey and I told him what Tyler had done. "You better talk to him," I said, "because I'm about ready to kill him." Well, I shouldn't have done that. Jeffrey went and talked to Tyler and he said, "If you ever lay a hand on Mama, I will beat the fire out of you." Tyler never raised his hand to me again, not even playing. He won't do it. He's scared of Jeffrey because Jeffrey became the man his daddy raised him to be, and he's trying to pass that on to Tyler.

As Tyler went through high school, he was involved in sports and he kept busy, and we got along fine. But, without strong memories of Johnny, he struggled to emulate him and he continued to try to follow Johnny's notorious legacy of his younger years. Tyler was kind of living large. Like his father, he liked to chase girls. He dated one girl for three years, pretty much all of high school. She kept him on a tight leash, and they were always together. Tyler said he didn't even know what a friend was while he dated her, since he spent all of his time with her. Later, when they broke up, he got very upset and then used his charm to go on a "girl spree."

Johnny's nickname was Fat Baby. Sometimes, people would come into the restaurant when Tyler was working and they'd take one look at Tyler and say, "Golly, you're Fat Baby's son, aren't you?" Tyler would feel so good about himself. "Yeah," he'd say. "I'm Fat Baby Junior." According to Tyler, it felt amazing. Other times, people would come in and say, "I know your mama and your dad." If Tyler knew that they were talking about Keith, he'd say "He ain't my daddy, he is my step-dad." He didn't want to be rude about it or to hurt Keith in any way, because Tyler loves Keith and respects him as a parental figure. "He'll never be my daddy," says Tyler. "I don't have one. Keith is a great stepdad and like a father, but I make a distinction between the two."

Jeffrey is a bit more flexible. He always introduced Keith as Keith or as his stepdad, but when he was being presented with an award or something like that, he would go ahead and let them refer to Keith as his dad instead of as his stepdad. "He has earned that right," Jeffrey said. "Because of how good he was to us." So, if someone flat out asked Jeffrey, "Is this your dad?" he would just say, "Yeah," or, if they're a friend, he'll explain that Keith is his stepdad.

Both of the boys respect and are proud of Keith for being the parent that he didn't have to be. And their distinction between dad and stepdad specifically is out of respect, love, pride, and honor for their father.

Always mature, Jeffrey approached the Hanna name differently than Tyler did. He always cared about what people thought of him, and he was careful never to do anything to jeopardize his name. Tyler was more inclined to take chances and have a good time, and he'd possibly be talked about, but Jeffrey taught him the importance of keeping his name—and the Hanna name—sacred.

It's interesting for Tyler, because he is like his daddy made over. I can remember when Johnny was a teenager and, then, to see Tyler the same age was remarkable. And, like Johnny, Tyler was into all this trouble and very mischievous. When he was young, Johnny did things that would make people say, "Why would he do something like that?" And Tyler is so much like that, every bit his daddy's son, with Johnny's playfulness and risk-taking.

I understood him, but Keith didn't so much.

Tyler and Keith would bump heads a lot. When they did, a lot of times Keith would turn right around and bring the problem to me. We had a lot of arguments about that. "You need to get on Tyler for this," Keith would say. "You need to get on Tyler for that."

I felt like Tyler was my son and I didn't want Keith to discipline him. If he needed a spanking, I would be the one to do it. "You know what?" I finally said. "I'm tired of you riding Tyler's back. If you don't have anything good that you can find about him, then don't talk to me about Tyler. Tyler is my son. I'll take care of Tyler."

That put more strain on our marriage. Each time, it would be tense for a couple weeks and then it would finally play out. Keith would come back to talk to me. "You do what you want to," he said. "Tyler is your son, but I'm telling you that you need to talk to him about that."

I would follow through and address the issue with Tyler, but part of me would also think that it wasn't fair when Keith backed off. When you have kids you have two parents, not just one. It would make me angry all over again because I felt like it was all on my shoulders. It was like I was a single mom. But then again, I caused most of it because I didn't want Keith to discipline him, and then I got angry when he wouldn't. I guess I wanted to have my cake and eat it too.

It was different with Jeffrey. When Keith and I first got married, Jeffrey put up a wall and wouldn't let Keith in at all. "You're not my dad," he said straight out. "You won't be my dad, so don't try to be." Keith didn't push. He did what he could and gave Jeffrey plenty of space, and eventually it all kind of fell into place. Eventually the two of them became really close.

As he grew up, Jeffrey emulated Johnny's adult persona more and more. He remained stoic and strong, always disciplined, in control, and eager to carry any burdens for Tyler and me. Johnny wanted his sons—especially Jeffrey—to truly learn that, when you get knocked down, you pull your big boy britches back up and you go right back. I wanted to make sure that I also instilled that in them, and I think I have. Jeffrey, especially, has Johnny's sense of discipline. He was always the kind of young man who would swallow hard and try to move on whenever he had a problem or if something sad happened to him. He would never whine to other people about his problems. In school, Jeffrey was always the person that other people would come to if they had a problem or needed to vent, and he would always help them work it out. He hardly ever vented to anybody else, except probably to Tosha.

No matter what, he did not ever want anyone to feel sorry for him. He always had the sense that there's somebody else, somewhere, who's had a hard time and who needs his support, so he didn't want the pity party on himself. He knew that he was strong, and that he would make it no matter what, so he saw himself as helping others, never as the person being helped. Even though he would feel sad sometimes, he didn't want to show his sadness. He wanted to be the rock. He wanted to allow Tyler and me to be sad, so he needed to be strong. He felt that if he was the rock, our lives would be a little better.

Once I married Keith, Jeffrey felt like I was taken care of. I was in good hands. But Jeffrey still felt responsible for Tyler, especially whenever the boys were off on their own—at school or out in the woods. Those situations reminded him of Johnny's murder, when it was just the two of them and there was no one but Jeffrey to take care of Tyler, to protect him and to make sure he did the right thing. Even after that, as Tyler grew up, Jeffrey knew that Tyler could hold his own, but Jeffrey still saw it as his job to make sure.

Like Johnny, Jeffrey was a very controlled person, disciplined and responsible all the time, except when he got mad. He struggled with it sometimes, feeling that he was too nice in some situations and, other times, like he got mad over the littlest thing. But, other than losing it when he was angry, Jeffrey thrived on control. That was his response to the murder and the helplessness he felt. To this day if he starts to feel helplessness, it bring tears to his eyes. Then, as quick as that, it'll switch to anger. If Jeffrey feels like he cannot control a situation or if he doesn't know what's going to happen, his eyes will water out of helplessness, and then get angry. Surprises were a problem for him. He felt like he could handle any situation, as long as he knew it was coming. So, as he became a man, he still didn't like situations where he could be blindsided. In fact, he continued to be marked by the terror of the murder, and has always been afraid to enter a house if he doesn't know who might be inside.

In 2007, Jeffrey and his girlfriend Tosha graduated from high school. Jeffrey decided to go to Tech School to complete his basic classes for college but, after a year, he decided that it would be better for him to join the Air Force and get his education there. With the wars in Iraq and Afghanistan I was very reluctant to accept his decision, but he joined.

One of the saddest days of my life by far was December 8, 2008, when Jeffrey left for San Antonio, Texas. I'm sure that I was feeling "empty nest syndrome," but it was bigger than that. I was so proud of Jeffrey and had come to depend on him so much. Although we never did talk about the day his daddy died, we did talk about his daddy quite often. Tyler looked up to Jeffrey as more than a brother, since Jeffrey filled the void. Keith, Tosha, my mom, Tyler, and Mot all drove Jeffrey to the recruiter's office to catch the bus to the airport. Half of my heart went with my son.

To make everything harder, the other half of my heart was with my own father. He had gotten sicker and it didn't look like he was going to get better. Mama was worn out trying to care for him, and my sister Sherri helped a lot.

I needed to do my part, but I couldn't stand to see Daddy suffer. I'm sure Sherri felt the same way. Finally, we called in Hospice. I also didn't know if I would be able to say good-bye to him. My daddy had been my rock, the one I leaned on the most when I needed someone to talk to about Johnny. I asked God to work a miracle, but God has His own ideas.

On December 20, 2008, twelve days after Jeffrey left for basic training, I was sitting next to Dad when he passed away. I was relieved that he was out of pain, but I hated to let him go. Many people had told me that I was just like him, and we'd had such a special connection after we lost Johnny. I felt like my heart was broken into a million pieces. I didn't know where I could find comfort, other than believing that Dad was with Johnny in heaven, watching over our family together.

It was hardest for Tyler. After he lost Johnny, Tyler turned to my dad as his most significant father figure. At the time he wasn't that close to Keith, so he took it hard when Dad died. From the time he was six-years-old, he felt like my dad was his daddy. It really hurt Tyler.

I hated to give Jeffrey news like that when he was down in San Antonio all by himself, but I called the Red Cross to tell him. Jeffrey was devastated but, true to form, he remained stoic and strong for Tyler and me. He couldn't come home for the funeral so I had to bury my Dad while my oldest son was hundreds of miles away from me, with only letters and occasional phone calls to connect us.

We knew that Jeffrey would not be home for Christmas that year so before he left for basic training we exchanged gifts with him. My dad presented Jeffrey with a gun that he'd had for a long time. "I want you to have this gun," Dad said. "Take care of it." I don't think another present would have been more monumental than Jeffrey getting one of my dad's guns, and my dad being able to give it to him.

When Jeffrey went off to basic, it was the first time he had ever been away from Tosha. One day, he called me. "Mom," he said, "I'm going to ask Tosha to marry me."

"Jeffrey," I said, "I think you should wait until you're done with basic training."

"No," he said. "I want to do it."

When I continued to protest, he told me that I needed to stay out of it.

I was devastated. It was really, really rough. It took me a while to admit that, instead of feeling the excitement or joy of "gaining a daughter," I felt like I was losing Jeffrey for good. Already he had gone away, and I wasn't going to be in a position to protect him anymore but, now, he wasn't going to be protecting me, either. I tried to be happy for him but I just couldn't let go, and I actually started resenting Tosha. I felt like I was losing Jeffrey and she was the reason why.

CHAPTER 28

"HANNA MEN"

WHEN JEFFREY GRADUATED from basic training, we went to see him. The whole family flew down to San Antonio. Tosha came. By this time, she and I had already had a few major fusses and Jeffrey was aware that things were not good between the two of us. She had a hard time understanding my position and I had a hard time understanding hers, so Jeffrey became the peacemaker.

In time I got used to Jeffrey not being home, and then I realized and accepted that all he was doing was what most grown men do: live his life with his new bride. As soon as I saw that what he wanted to do was so normal, my relationship with Tosha changed dramatically. I lost all resentment as I realized that she was exactly what Jeffrey needed.

Tosha's father had died in a car wreck when she was little, just three years old. At that time, her dad actually had custody of her and then, after she lost him, her grandparents raised her. She and Jeffrey shared a lot of the same beliefs and they really clicked. He liked how feisty she was but found her sweet at the same time. They knew each other really well and enjoyed each other's company a lot. They had been best friends for years.

One day in April 2009, when Tosha was in San Antonio, Jeffrey took her for a ride in a horse carriage. He asked her to close her eyes and then he opened his backpack. He pulled out a plush Air Force "Build-a-Bear" and a glass frame that had a poem in it. He put the poem in her hands, told her to open her eyes, and asked her to read the poem. While she read aloud, Jeffrey pressed a button to activate a recorder inside the bear which said, "Tosha, will you marry me?" Just then, she read the last line of the poem: "Will you marry me?"

Surprised, she cried, "Yes!"

Their wedding was on June 6, two months later. They both wanted an outdoor wedding and it was a beautiful but really hot afternoon, about ninety-five degrees. The wedding was at a college in Tosha's town. To the hundred guests it was lovely, though Tosha was stressed because she felt like it wasn't perfect. The music skipped some at the beginning and a loud motorcycle rode by during a prayer. They had applied for and received their marriage license, but forgot to bring it to the ceremony so the preacher could sign it. Tosha's aunt knew someone who could go to the courthouse to get it, and they ended up signing it at the reception. Jeffrey spent the wedding trying to get Tosha to relax.

For me it was a hard day, not because I had any problems with Tosha—those feelings were long gone—but because Johnny should have been there. Just like Jeffrey's graduation, the wedding was another big family event to happen after we lost Johnny and I was so aware of his absence. Tyler stood up as Jeffrey's best man and I sat there looking up at them and thinking, *It isn't fair. That is so not fair.* As hard as it was for me, I realized that it wasn't the same for the boys. I know that Jeffrey would have given anything for his daddy to be at his wedding, to be standing up there beside him, but I also know that he didn't dwell on that on the most important day of his life. I did.

At the wedding, Jeffrey and Tosha had a table set to the side where they had a special display of some flowers, dedicated to their fathers. I was touched by that. Jeffrey said that he wished that he and Tosha could have met each other's fathers, but she jokes that she's married to Johnny because

I've told her how much Jeffrey acts like his father.

I know that people see Tosha as my daughter-in-law, but I feel like she has become my daughter.

After the wedding Jeffrey and Tosha moved to Georgia, where he was stationed. Living in Warner Robins, a few hours from me and from all of their family members, they learned to rely on each other. Their relationship grew very strong.

"Sheila," Tosha said one day. "Do you know that Jeffrey tells me he loves me every time that he talks to me, every time he leaves?"

I told her the reason behind it, explaining that after Johnny died we always said "I love you" when we are saying goodbye.

"That is so neat," she said. And now she is careful to say it too, every time.

I wish we'd started that in our family before Johnny died.

I'd give anything to have one more chance to make sure he knew how much I loved him. I want him to know that, when I argued with him about not giving me forty dollars, that it really didn't mean that much to me. I would like to talk about all the stupid times that we argued, and let him know that I never would have argued had I known. If I only could have seen in that crystal ball what was going to happen, whatever was so important to argue over would have meant nothing to me. I think that we take things for granted that the people we love will be there tomorrow, and it takes something bad to happen, like Johnny getting killed, before we realize that you have to tell people how much you appreciate them and how much you love them. You are not always given the chance again. If Johnny would have been sick—like if he had cancer and we went through weeks and weeks of knowing that he wasn't going to live—he would have known without a doubt how much I really loved him. But the way that he was taken, I know that he knows that I loved him but I don't know if he knew how much.

That summer, I planned a ten-year memorial for August 6. I wanted to give the boys an opportunity to celebrate Johnny's life, and another way to overcome their loss. It was a lovely evening. Our preacher spoke, of course, as well as the sheriff and chief and we had nice music. I took this opportunity to acknowledge and express our gratitude to all the emergency responders, law enforcement, crimestoppers, the community and all our family and friends that helped us. It was also the time I shared personal home videos. I wanted the people who attended to see the real Johnny with his family and show that he is not just a name on a crime report or obituary. We also had an open floor, with remembrances.

At one point, I looked out in the pews and saw Jeffrey and Tyler sobbing. They were overcome by emotion and crying hard. I felt sick, filled with regret. I thought that I had messed up by having the service, so right then I told everybody that this would be the last time that I would ever hold a community service for Johnny.

As soon as the ceremony ended, I talked to Jeffrey and Tyler. They told me that it was a cathartic opportunity to honor their father, and they appreciated it. They told me that they were grateful.

It's hard to believe that it had been ten years since we lost Johnny. In some ways, everything had changed. In other ways, nothing had. I was still even having the recurring dream that had started about a month after Johnny died, about Johnny abandoning the boys. Other times, I was completely asleep, dreaming about Johnny, when I'd wake up and think Keith was Johnny lying beside me. That was hard. I wish I knew if this was going to keep going on forever. Will I ever get over those dreams? Will I ever quit having them? I think the dreams continue because his death still doesn't make sense to me.

When Tyler graduated from high school in 2011 it was another hard time for me, one of those momentous family occasions when I was so aware that Johnny should have been there. Even after high school, Tyler is still reliving his daddy's younger years. He idolizes the image of Johnny as a fun, partying guy, and he relishes the stories he's heard about Johnny's wild years. Tyler is proud to be a Hanna and is proud of who his daddy was, and he has latched on to Johnny's high school legacy, I'm afraid, because he doesn't have any of those memories of his own. He said he just can't remember. He loves to hear the stories, but doesn't want to be asked about what he remembers. There just isn't much for him to share, and he feels ashamed of that. "It makes me feel like people think since I'm his son that I should remember, but I don't," he said. "That's my daddy. I should remember him."

I am saddened that Tyler has lost those memories, but I'm grateful that he blocked out the memories of the horrors of seeing his daddy's bloody body in his own house.

Jeffrey remembers all of it.

It hurts me more than anything that the boys' daddy was taken from them, and it is so much worse that they had to see what they saw. With Tyler, he lost a lot of that memory as time went by, which is good for him, I think. But on the flip side not only did he lose that memory, he lost the memories that he and his dad made. He lost his knowledge of his father. With Jeffrey the bad thing is that he remembers what he saw that day, but the good side is that he also remembers his life with Johnny before that day. Good and bad. You trade one for the other, and you live with both.

This past year, I was in Texas for a conference, and I was coming home on August 6. I went to bed the night before thinking that the next day would be good, since I was going home. I got up that morning and the first thing that popped into my brain was "the anniversary." I was on the shuttle from my hotel to the airport when Jeffrey sent me a text, "Thinking of you today. Be careful. Love you." Now, it's not unusual for Jeffrey to text me, but not that kind of sentimental text. I felt that he must be having a hard time, so I texted back, "I'm fine. How are you doing today?" He said he was fine, and the conversation went on from there. Then I texted Tyler. I didn't hear anything back from him, so I worried that he might be having an emotionally rough day. I texted him again with details of when I'd be getting home—and, of course, I said "I love you." He responded, "I love you, too. See you when you get home."

Different boys. Different memories. Different ways to cope with the memories.

When I lost Johnny, I lost my best friend. I also lost my home. Even though it wasn't taken from us, they might as well have taken it because none of us ever felt comfortable there again. And I keep it, because I can't let it go.

It was the same way for Marshall and the house where Barbara died. He had that house forever. That was the house where Johnny's parents lived, where they raised their three children. But, after Barbara went off to the garden behind the out-building and took her own life, the place was never the same. Marshall remarried and lives with his second wife, Thelma, but he still owns the old house. It sits there, vacant.

Over the years, I've rented out our house on Hilley Road, because I can't let it go. At the same time, it's hard for us to even go in there. There are certain places in the house—like the laundry room and the back porch—where I just can't be, even though I never saw Johnny lying there myself. I still imagine what Johnny looked like, and I feel horrified to be there.

To this day, when I have to go near that room, I still picture Johnny lying there, over the laundry room threshold, his body half inside, half outside. The same is true for the boys.

We always knew that Jeffrey had seen the murder scene, and that, all those years, he had to live with that image and those details. Plus, he was old enough to understand. On the other hand, we just thought that Tyler had to adjust to realizing that his dad wasn't coming back. We thought that Tyler had to cope for a while. All these years, we didn't know that he had seen the bloodbath. He did, but he didn't talk about it for more than ten years.

When we started working on the book and talking about the past, Tyler and Jeffrey compared notes and Tyler told Jeffrey that, when his brother went to call 911, Tyler went and looked. He saw it.

Interestingly, Tyler's recollection of it was completely different from Jeffrey's. It makes sense. Since Jeffrey walked over to the laundry room thinking that he needed to close the door, he walked around that corner focused on the door at the far end of the room. His perception went from the open door, to Johnny's feet, up his body, to his chest, to his hand, the blade, and then to Johnny's face, which was surrounded by that deep pool of blood. It was as if Jeffrey had tunnel vision, looking at his father's face surrounded by a red halo. He didn't see anything else. Instantly, he was out of there.

But, seeing Jeffrey's reaction, Tyler went around that corner assuming that ladybugs must have been all over the walls. As he turned to look, he focused on the walls, which is why he saw blood, everywhere—on the washer and dryer, the cupboards, the ceiling, all of the walls, and all over Johnny's clothes—such that Tyler did not even know what Johnny had been wearing.

When the boys recently talked about it, it was the first time that Jeffrey realized that Tyler had looked. None of us ever knew.

Tyler, in contrast, doesn't mind being in the house and he wants us to keep it. "It makes me happy to know that I'm on my daddy's land," he says. "I know that my daddy worked this land and I've always wanted to work this land and to live here." One time, he asked me why we didn't just stay there instead of moving. "I don't really believe in paranormal stuff," he recently said. "But, anyway, it's my daddy and my daddy ain't going to do nothing to me but watch over me, so, if anything, I feel safer with him here." That said, Tyler is still a little hesitant. He admits that, if he were to spend much time inside the house, he'd dwell on what happened to Johnny, and it would probably give him nightmares about murderers attacking him.

Over the years, as landlords, we occasionally had to go into the house to take care of maintenance, problems, and whatever came up with the property. Tyler had been there three or four times after the murder and he does fine. But Jeffrey is still uneasy. As the years went by, it bothered him when he had to go inside, especially if he had to go back toward the laundry room. Now, he goes in to do what he's got to do and he gets out. "If I just went in there and sat down, it probably would start bothering me," he said.

"I reckon I'd turn it over in my mind and get myself to an exit so I could feel normal again."

Just as he did in the first few months after Johnny died, Jeffrey continued to fear walking into a house or a quiet room. While his fear was terrible right after the murder, he still to this day is on alert whenever he goes into a house. Next to losing his daddy, this feeling of vulnerability has been the worst burden of his experience. Even in his own house, he can feel unsafe and will be super cautious. Sometimes, when he is in a situation that causes him to fear for himself, he has a flash of the image of Johnny dead, as he considers that the same thing could happen to him. His home in Georgia is in a subdivision, with close neighbors, so he doesn't feel as uneasy. But whenever he arrives at home, he checks out the entire house, room by room. He and Tosha keep the doors locked, even when they are at home and, in the evening, he has to have all of the blinds closed because otherwise he feels like someone outside might be watching him. He also has a fence around his backyard and good security. Still, at nighttime, he sometimes psychs himself out and gets to thinking that somebody could be outside. To make it worse, a few break-ins have occurred recently near his home, so he is extremely alert when coming home.

If Jeffrey lived out in the country, like in our old neighborhood, his fear would be more bothersome and he would feel more vulnerable. In a remote house, Jeffrey is always aware that someone could have gotten in without anyone knowing. For him, if something surprises him to give him an adrenaline rush, he says it's the worst feeling in the world. This makes him feel just like he did the day he turned the corner and found his daddy.

We can't let the old house go because of our memories and connection to it. We have to be content with each other and with our memories because life and home and family, as we knew it, is no more.

Now the house is run down and sad. Johnny took so much pride in what we had built on the land, but now his vegetable garden is all grown over with weeds and shrubs. The lawn is weedy and rough, and the Johnny Quills don't come up anymore.

CHAPTER 29
FINDING DADDY

THOUGH I WORKED hard to find the capacity for forgiveness inside my heart and mind, my sons had not. They were nowhere near even being interested in forgiving Otis or the other suspects. They were much more consumed with revenge than with reconciliation, more interested in justice than acceptance. "I'm not a very forgiving person," Jeffrey states with determination in his voice.

Of course, all three of us have experienced obstacles to forgiveness and acceptance. For Tyler, one of the hardest issues was that at least some of the murderers—Otis, for one—knew Johnny personally. Having been in fights, Tyler understood how confrontations can occur; how for men, fights sometimes just happen. But in Tyler's experience, it was no good if he got into a fight with a guy that he knew because he'd feel guilty if he got carried away and fought an acquaintance. He didn't have so many regrets if he got into a fight against somebody at another school, someone he didn't know. Then it was okay.

To Tyler, Johnny's death would have stung less if the killers had been strangers, some guys who drove down from North Carolina or some creeps from the drug corridor—anyone who had just driven by a random house that they decided to rob. But Johnny's death was not random. Otis, Shane, and Robert either knew Johnny or their family knew Johnny. And Otis knew Johnny pretty well. After all, his daughter went to school with Johnny's son! Tyler could not comprehend how Otis could ignore that relationship when he was killing Johnny.

Since they did it anyway, Tyler felt like it made the murder even more horrible, more evil. As bad as Tyler felt if he got into a scrape with a friend, he couldn't imagine how anyone could rob someone they knew, much less kill someone. "That's just so wrong," Tyler says, "on all different levels."

It crossed our minds that Otis's wife, Angel, might also have been at the robbery when Johnny died. I always suspected her, too, because I doubted that any man would steal makeup and family movies. Also, Angel seemed to recognize Sherri's jewelry box in the back of the police car when the police first talked to her and Otis. Why would she have reacted to that box? Maybe she was afraid to get near it because it looked just like my stolen jewelry box.

Tyler couldn't bring himself to see Angel as guilty. He acknowledges that she might have been in on it, but he tends to envision her as a thief—rummaging through our stuff or sitting outside in the truck. "I don't see her doing anything to my daddy," he says.

Another longstanding obstacle to our ability to accept and move on was, of course, the justice system. After more than a dozen years since Johnny was murdered, only one man has been held responsible, despite clear evidence that more than one person had killed Johnny. Whether it was Shane Rice and Robert Compton—or not—it was somebody. The need for justice has remained with all of us, and it always will, because justice represents a validation that Johnny's life was worth holding someone—everyone—responsible. The lack of justice is always hard.

"The justice system hasn't done anything for me," Tyler says. "It aggravates the mess outta me." Part of it was that Tyler felt that Otis should have been killed for what he'd done. "The way I see it, he took a life, he should have his life taken," Tyler says.

Jeffrey, too, believes in the death penalty, "but I don't like it," he says. "I think that you should die the way you killed the person. If you shoot somebody, you should be shot. If you stab somebody, you should be stabbed."

I don't think that would have been enough for Tyler. "I want to get my revenge," he adds. "No matter what they do to him, that's not my revenge." Tyler thinks about the suspects and believes that, one day, they'll "get what's coming to 'em." I know that, if he were to run into any of them, he'd want to beat them up. "I wouldn't want to kill him, kill him," he says. "But I'd beat him so bad. And every time I hit him I would tell him how I felt and ask him questions. Why would you do that to somebody that's never done anything to your family? How would he feel if he was in my shoes, if he was a young kid and somebody killed his daddy? How would he feel?"

People have asked Jeffrey if he would kill Otis or the other suspects if he had the chance. "Heck no, I wouldn't kill him," Jeffrey says. "I don't want him to go out easy. I would probably do everything except pull the shot to the head, because I wouldn't want to kill him. I would want him to suffer, to be miserable the rest of his life."

When Jeffrey hears himself, though, he questions his feelings. "Wow," he says. "That makes me sound like a mean, mean person."

In a perfect world, Jeffrey says, the killers' suffering should be equal to what happened to Johnny. Like Tyler, Jeffrey believes that the "same thing that happened to Dad should happen to them, that way it will be equal on both sides." But, Jeffrey adds, "I honestly don't think that I would feel completely better if the same thing happened to them. I think I would feel better if I were to get a chance to fight them, legally."

That's important to Jeffrey. My boys are definitely not the kind of men who would go break the law for their own emotional gratification, and Jeffrey has articulated this, saying that he is not vengeful enough to break laws to get his revenge. But if he could do it legally, he would. "If they come in and the cops said, 'We'll put you all in this little cage right here and you can do whatever you want without getting in trouble,' I'd do it in a heartbeat. But I'm not going to go break laws to do it. I'm not that vengeful."

If the police finally get the evidence to convict other suspects and they end up spending their lives in jail, would that satisfy my sons? Would that be enough?

"It has to be," says Jeffrey. "If it was a perfect world, I would like them to suffer just as much as my daddy and the rest of us suffered. I would want them to have physical and medical conditions that make them miserable and emotional pain, guilt, for what they did." By itself, Jeffrey feels, jail is not punishment enough. "Nobody really suffers in jail. Jail just keeps them from hurting everybody else. They don't really make them suffer any."

I know, Jeffrey and Tyler are young men, and I think that their feelings and thoughts about revenge are something they have to do to cope because, among other things, they feel let down by society's justice. So I understand that they have that emotional need. I don't like it, but I understand it.

Another obstacle to healing has been our other losses along the way. Of course, my dad died, and that was really hard. Dad was Jeffrey and Tyler's first father figure after Johnny, and he was extremely close to the boys, especially because we lived with them for a short time after Johnny died.

The boys continued to visit Marshall and Barbara regularly and felt close to their daddy through his parents. So, when Barbara died, it was like they lost part of the direct link to their dad. The stories, pictures, and memories that Barbara used to share with the boys were gone in a blink of an eye. They knew that her death was a direct result of losing her son, their daddy.

We also lost Stuart, Mot's husband. Throughout my sons' lives, they were very close to Stuart, and they had a special relationship. He was like another grandfather, until he suddenly died.

Both of my boys have also experienced the deaths of close friends, and those incidents brought up all of their grief, all over again. When he was a teenager Jeffrey lost his best friend, who took his own life. It was desperately hard for Jeffrey, and his grief was raw and overwhelming. It was one of the few times that Tyler and I ever saw Jeffrey cry. Tyler, too, recently lost a friend who fell asleep at the wheel and hit a tree on his way home from work. I know that grief is part of life, and it is always hard for young people, but for my boys, there's a deeper sadness associated with death. With every loss in life, they have to wade through it, again and again.

Of all the deaths they have experienced, only one of them was foreseeable. The others were unexpected. For the boys, they have learned to prepare for death, but they are never ready for it. Some of the preparation comes out when they tell the people they love that they love them before leaving or hanging up a phone. At the same time, I also realize that I was in my thirties before I lost anyone close to me, but the boys had lost several people who they were close to by the age of sixteen. I understand that death is a part of life, but I think it takes on a whole new meaning for my boys. To them death is normal and accepted.

Life is like that, I think. Whatever our histories are, each of us has to deal with our own baggage. As much as we try to overcome it, it comes back from time to time. All we can do is recognize it.

Even though forgiveness has been hard to come by, I'm pleased that both of my sons have a Christian foundation that include personal relationships with God. I believe that this will get them through all that has happened in their lives—and whatever is to come for them.

Jeffrey goes to church and enjoys it, but he finds it a bit boring at times and then he doesn't want to be there, especially when he feels that a preacher is speaking mostly to the older folks. If Jeffrey can't relate to a preacher's sermon, the service doesn't interest him. "It's not about me going to church and hanging out with all the churchgoers," he says. "I don't get down on my knees and do all this, but I do have a relationship with God. I talk to Him and I pray to Him and we have our own relationship." Before he goes to bed at night, he says his prayers. Before he eats a meal, he says his prayers. And he'll pray anytime, even walking around shopping or driving down the road, if he feels like it. "I just start talking to God," he says.

"It don't matter who you are," Jeffrey says. "If you go through any kind of military training, you're going to find religion because you ain't got anybody to talk to for nine, ten, twelve weeks. Nobody cares about you when you're there, so you want somebody to care for you, and you got to talk to somebody." For Jeffrey, growing up around God, he turned to religion.

But in terms of church, he's not as "hard core" as a lot of us, including Tosha. After her dad died, she was raised by grandparents who took her to church every weekend and she still has a vibrant and cherished church life—sometimes with Jeffrey.

Tyler's faith journey was completely different. After losing his daddy when he was six-years-old, he was angry with God. It took time, but Tyler came to understand that Johnny's death wasn't God's fault. He also says that "God has a reason for it, even though I don't know it. Nobody knows it but Him," Tyler adds. "But we will one day." Still, he fights his anger. "I guess you've just got to forgive and forget," he says. "It's hard to do it. I have not forgiven them, but I have forgiven God."

When Johnny, Jeffrey, and I were baptized, Tyler was too young. He remembers being scared of the water at that time, fearing that he would drown. His fear was practical, not spiritual, and he was obviously too young to make a commitment to God. If he had, he would have just been doing what everybody else in his family was doing. Years later Tyler was baptized, though he continues to grapple with his faith. "I have had second thoughts on my baptism," he admits, "but I have asked God into my heart too many times to count because I want to make sure I live for Him, and to make sure that He is with me."

Though the boys are not yet able to forgive, I'm pleased that they work on their anger, and that this is something their faith helps them deal with. "I think He takes away most of my anger," Tyler says. "Whenever I'm talking about Him, I'm mellowing out and everything is fine. I want Him in my heart," he adds, "because I know that Christians say that God teaches them the right way and if I didn't have God in my heart, I would not be like I am now."

My sons have good lives now. They are proud of what they have and how they live their lives, because they work hard to be the kind of men they are. That's an important value in our family, something that Johnny taught them. His memory continues to teach them this, and so do the men in our family. Marshall always told the boys, "Just make sure people know what you stand for, and that you stand for what you want to stand for."

To the boys, that sums it up. "You want to do the right things," Jeffrey says. "You want to be somebody that is known for working hard, earning everything he has, taking care of his family, being a good man. Even at work..." he adds. "Say Tyler joins the Air Force. I don't want him to join and have a former supervisor say, 'Oh, you're a Hanna? You related to Jeff? Are you going to be a dirt bag?' I want them to say, 'You're going to be a good troop.'"

Tyler has the same standards, because Jeffrey was his number-one role model for nearly all of his life. Like a father figure, Jeffrey still has a great influence on Tyler. "I look up to Jeffrey, even today," Tyler says. "Jeffrey is the person that I want to be like." Tyler feels wonderful when he makes Jeffrey proud. If he fears that something would get Jeffrey mad or upset, he'll try not to do it, and if he thinks Jeffrey will applaud an action or a decision, then he'll do it. "He has a heavy influence on me," Tyler says with Johnny's smile.

In one particular way, though, Tyler feels he can't measure up to Jeffrey: Jeffrey doesn't cry, and Tyler wears his heart on his sleeve. "I'd rather be like him," Tyler says. "I feel sissified and downgraded." Like Jeffrey, Tyler believes that he shouldn't cry, even if he's in unbearable physical pain, though that could be the only exception. "I don't think anybody should cry," says Tyler. "I don't know what tears are for. It don't make you feel any better and it makes you look bad." Being a very physical guy, Tyler can endure significant physical pain and probably wouldn't cry over something physical. "But you get to talking about my feelings and I get all emotional," he says, "and I hate that. I want to make sure that I'm there for my family, when the time comes and they need me to be strong for them." While he wishes he was different, he also knows that he is who he is. "I ain't going to be able to change that," he says. "I know I am the way I am, but I don't like it. Then again, I do think it's good that I'm able to express my emotions. I'm happy but I ain't. I wish I was like Jeffrey."

Though he's conflicted about expressing his emotion, Tyler is confident of himself as a man. "I know I'm my daddy's son and I honestly think I will be able to be there for my family if something happens," he says. "I'll be there for my family first and then my emotions can come last."

Jeffrey is another story. He holds in his feelings, ultimately concerned that they not be a burden on anyone else. It's hard for him to share what he feels and that has been an issue with Tosha, who wishes that he would share more. But Jeffrey took on the responsibility as the man of the house when he was ten- years-old, and he still does not like to show his feelings or let on that anything is bothering him.

As the years have gone by, we've watched Tyler learn about and emulate the child side of Johnny, sometimes longing to be more like the adult version of Johnny, like Jeffrey. On the flip side, Jeffrey always related to Johnny's adult side, so he never sought to imitate his father's fun side. As he has become his own man, though, he seems to be having more fun. While he is still almost always a mature, serious, and strong man, when it's time to have fun, Jeffrey can let loose. He'll relax with his friends, sing karaoke, and enjoy a few beers. When he's like that, he's really fun. "Until you make him mad," Tyler says. "Then he'll beat the fire out of you."

Though anger remains an issue for both of my boys, they believe they come by it honestly, not from the murder. After all, that's the way Johnny was. He was a Hanna, and they are Hannas. As Tyler says, "I'm just angry a lot. If I think about anything with my daddy's murder or other things that have happened in my life that upset me, I get very, very angry. I don't get as much upset, as I get angry," he adds, "because I don't understand, I guess, and I hate not being able to understand something." For Tyler, thinking about God or talking about Him helps him to forget his anger.

Jeffrey, too, feels a great deal of anger, but he also thinks that it's in his genes, not the result of August 6, 1999. "I don't think I'm angry because of that," he says. "But, other than love for my wife and family, of course, the emotion I would say that I feel the most would be anger." He adds that he is a pretty happy person most of the time and definitely has a lot of joy in his life, but he explains that he doesn't feel sad very often, because sadness automatically turns into anger. "When Daddy died," he explained, "obviously I was sad, but I was more angry, like something needed to be done. I want my chance to fix this." Whatever his anger is about, it is often directed at Johnny's killers. "They were cowards not to go man-to-man," he says, "even though they had him way outnumbered. I don't know if I would be as mad if it had been a fair fight."

All these years after Johnny died, I never stopped questioning my parenting, or doubting my decisions as a mother. I never knew if it was right or wrong to let Jeffrey act so much like a grown-up, and I never knew how to help Tyler keep his memories. Sometimes, I felt real regret about my decisions. Other times, I just felt so sad, wondering what kind of men they would have been if they'd had Johnny until he was an old man. But, then, I look at my sons. I know that I could not have had any better boys, because my boys are great, and they are doing well.

I see the smiles on their faces when they talk to each other, see the laughter when they goof around. And that's when I remember: Everything happened the way it should have happened.

These days, Tyler and Keith have a good relationship. They still bump heads, but Keith is more of a father figure, though he will sometimes take up for Tyler against me. In a way, I think that they have the best relationship that you can expect from a stepdad and stepson. I think that's fair.

Keith and I continue to have some difficulties because I still mourn Johnny, but I am able to control it better now. I realized it is a constant effort for me to move forward and quit allowing my past to dictate my future.

Keith and I have been married eleven years now. Johnny and I were only married seven. Still, Johnny was such a big part of my life—the second big crush of my life and my first true love. I won't ever get over him, though I have learned to cope. And I have learned not to take life and love for granted.

I also have a renewed passion for my job, though it took several years for me to find it again after what happened. Actually, now, I am probably more passionate than I ever was in the past, because I have personally lived through the type of call that only happens to "other people."

Jeffrey and Tosha are doing well on their own, and they have a beautiful little house in Georgia. Still in the Air Force, Jeffrey works in military security, which means that his job is as a policeman. The Air Force told him what careers were open to him and he chose security because he can't stand to sit at a desk and do paperwork, but has to be doing things. He says he'd like to be a street cop or detective, his contribution toward justice for the injustices. He realizes that such work would definitely put his feelings and anger to the test, but he feels sure that he has the self-control to be a good police office. For now, while he's in the Air Force, he works in security forces, guarding airplanes and other military resources, as well as providing police services.

In his job, he has had to deal with some marijuana crimes, never any drugs harder than that. And, so far, he's never had to respond to a theft, which usually only occurs at the base supply store, which is like a Wal-Mart. Jeffrey doesn't have as much of an emotional problem with shoplifting as he does when someone steals from an individual who has worked hard for what he has.

In all aspects of his life, Jeffrey has kept the horror of losing his father as a very private incident. Very few people who know him know what happened, because he still does not want the pity party, and he's generally very private. "I don't want anybody to know anything about me that they don't need to know," he says.

Taking after his father as a disciplined and responsible man, Jeffrey is on a good start in life. He has moved up quickly in his Air Force career, winning awards, gaining responsibility, and earning credentials. He is also like his father in that he is a good and compassionate man. Though he can be coldhearted with people who have no regard for their fellow man, Jeffrey will do anything for a friend—and that includes any good and decent human being. Like his father, he is a generous friend, the embodiment of his father's moral character.

"When Jeffrey started dating Tosha, I asked around to find out what I could about him," said Gordon, Tosha's grandfather. "I was told that as long as Tosha was with Jeffrey, I wouldn't have to worry about anyone hurting her. That person was exactly right and I have not had to worry about her well-being since." Jeffrey said that, when he heard Gordon make that statement, it was the proudest moment of his life, a confirmation for Jeffrey that he was leading the life that his daddy would be proud of and becoming a man just like his daddy.

Tyler is like a Johnny clone, and he loves it. "I love meeting somebody and before I even introduce myself, they say they know that I'm Fat Baby's son," Tyler beams. "I wouldn't have it any other way." Like Johnny, Tyler is a spitfire—fun, funny, friendly. He played football in high school and continues to follow his father's footsteps as everybody's buddy. Emulating his father's gregarious personality is effortless for Tyler, who recently started college.

As they have grown from boys to men, Jeffrey and Tyler—each in his own way—have come to emulate and own Johnny's character and stature as a man. In a way, they are each a part of Johnny, living on in the way they live their lives.

"I felt like he was a real good dad," Jeffrey says. "I guess everybody feels that way about their parents, and I guess I feel the same way as everybody else."

That makes me happy to no end, because that's all I've ever really wanted for my boys. But, at the same time, I also wanted them to always remember him, and to bring him with them as they went through their lives. I feel that they have done that.

"I remember thinking that, no matter what happened, Daddy could fix anything," says Jeffrey. "I remember thinking that he was the strongest person I know, and the fastest person. Just like everybody else, I thought he was superman."

Jeffrey remembers that Johnny would race him and win, every single time. Jeffrey would cry, but Johnny would still beat him. Johnny wouldn't just let him win, but Jeffrey had to earn it, for real. "If I could see him now," Jeffrey says, "I would want to race and wrestle him in the yard to see if he could still handle me with no problem." This is another trait that Jeffrey uses to pass onto Tyler.

In time, my boys will have their own children, and then we will see who handles whom. Since Jeffrey is already married, I don't imagine it'll be too long before he becomes a father, and sometimes I wonder what kind of dad he will be.

"I hope I'm going to be just like him," he says.

I hope so, too.

ACKNOWLEDGEMENTS

I WANT TO THANK the following people: Jeffrey and Tyler Hanna, my precious boys, the reason I keep going. Thank you for standing with me and helping me though this process. I am thankful that this gave us an opportunity to open up, and share tears and laughter. You gave me strength and encouraged me when I needed it, and that meant so much to me. I love you more than words could ever say and I am so proud of both of you!

Keith Wiles, the man who has stood beside me through thick and thin. I know this has not been an easy journey for you, but you stayed right there beside me and I am forever thankful. I thank you for being my best friend first and then my husband. Thank you for being the father you didn't have to be to Jeffrey and Tyler. You were the glue that I needed to mend my broken heart. As we continue to walk through this life together, I want you to know that God couldn't have sent a better person for me to stand beside and conquer whatever comes our way. You mean so much to me and I love you from the bottom of my heart!

To my mom, Sue Parnell, thank you for always being there to listen to me and encourage me when I needed it the most, and for opening your house to me and the boys after Johnny died. Your unselfish actions made a big difference in my life today and I am forever grateful to you. I love you!

Marshall Hanna, thank you for making me keep my eyes upon the Lord even when I didn't really want to. You have endured so much pain but you never failed to share your love and encouragement with me. You have always treated me like a daughter and I thank you for that. I love you!

To my pastor, Fred Griggs, for not giving up on me when I had given up on myself. As I have often said, you have prayed for me more than any person I know and it was those prayers and your guidance that put me back on the straight and narrow way. Thank you so much! I love you!

Jennifer Burdette, I am so glad that I got to work with you on this book. Your God-given talent of photography shows in each of the pictures in the book. Thank you for sharing your talent and making the book come to life. I love you!

Amanda Bindel, Tony Vecchio, Erika Block, and Michael Wright, thank you for your tireless effort and God-given talent of helping with the creation of the book. Your patience was surely tested trying to get everything completed before deadlines and I know it was hard but you made it look so easy. Thank you so much!

Megan Trank, thank you for keeping me straight and focused on what needed to be done. I knew God would send an angel to help finish this book and that is what he did when you came along. Thank you very much!

Tony Kaufman, thank you for the legal guidance and direction. Without you this book would have never been released so thank you so much!!

Katie Vecchio, thank you, for giving so much energy to this book when I know you were not feeling well. You are truly the rock behind this book and I appreciate you so much for sharing your writing talent with me and the rest of the world. Love you!

Tracy Ertl, thank you for believing in my story and taking a chance on me. For your endless dedication in making sure that the book was exactly the way I wanted it and guiding me through the process, I am forever thankful. Love you!

To my family, Johnny's family, and our friends, thank you for always being there for me and the boys before, during, and after: Sherri and Doug Hill, James and Kristie Parnell, Ken and Lynn Waters, Marshall and Thelma Hanna, Wanda Butler, Tommy and Gayle Brown, Tracy and Angie Hanna. Oh, my goodness, there are so many of you that I am thankful for that I can't list them all and I certainly don't want to miss anyone, so I want to thank the Lowndesville, Iva, and Calhoun Falls Communities that prayed for us, visited us, provided pertinent information to law enforcement, or helped us to overcome and work on healing. Love you!

To the Abbeville Sherriff's Office and, more specifically, Sheriff Goodwin, Chief Johnson, Detective David Alford, and the other officers and victim advocates who were instrumental in the investigation or taking the time to listen to me. Thank you for everything. I know you spent many sleepless nights working this case and I will be forever grateful. You taught me patience and persistence. And because of this, I know that I won't stop pursuing my effort to make sure everyone involved is held accountable.

To the Calhoun Falls Rescue Squad, specifically Stan and Jan Johnson and Darrell Manning. Thank you so much for taking care of my boys until I got there that day. I know you went above and beyond your call of duty and I am so appreciative. Thank you!

To Christi and Keisha from Abbeville 911, thank you for everything you did that day. I can only imagine how hard this call was for you. I know too well about the stress you encounter from everyday calls for service, and then to receive this call from Jeffrey must have really taken its toll on you. I appreciate what you did and how you held it together to get help for my family that day. Love you!

To Julie Ray, thank you for believing in me and being the person that started the wheels turning on this project. It never would have happened if it wasn't for you. I love you and appreciate you so much!

—*Sheila Hanna-Wiles*

S HEILA, JEFFREY, AND TYLER trusted me to be their storyteller. They showed great courage in opening their hearts, revealing their secrets, and sharing the story of the most difficult moments of their lives. The results are a meaningful book and a valuable friendship, for which I'm grateful.

I appreciate publisher Tracy Ertl, whose faith in me gets me past the rough spots. She also hires good people like Michael Wright and Erika Block, and I'm grateful for them, too. We couldn't have finished this book on time without Amanda Bindel, a wonderful wordsmith who bailed me out when my body failed me; I'll always be grateful for her tenacity, work ethic, and way with words, and I look forward to working with her again.

Finally, I thank the best parents in the world, Ken and Nancy Clark, whose love and support helped get me though a tough stretch, and Tony, Nick, and Sophie Vecchio, who put up with seemingly endless delayed gratification. We're getting there!

—Katie Clark Vecchio